'The young homeless ma
study, demonstrating t
vulnerability, and bringing
it illustrates the ways in whi
improve their life chances, ₁ _____ ₜₕₑᵢᵣ ᵢₙᵢₜᵢₐₗ disadvantages. Essential
reading for those concerned to tackle the housing crisis, with policy
implications for social justice agendas and young people more widely too.'

**Marjorie Mayo, Emeritus Professor of Community Development,
Goldsmiths, University of London**

'In this standout text, Tina Byrom and Sheine Peart give authentic voice to
the insights and experiences of homeless youth. Through a careful blend of
grounded empirical analysis and innovative theoretical perspectives, they
not only bring homeless young people's harrowing and traumatic struggles
to life but also provide a positive vision of cross-agency actions needed to
resolve the issues. Carefully researched and accessibly written, the book is
a must-read for those seeking to understand the multiple and underlying
social and cultural factors that underpin youth homelessness.'

**Ross Deuchar, Professor of Criminology and Assistant Dean,
University of the West of Scotland**

Young and Homeless

Young and Homeless

Exploring education, life experiences and aspirations of homeless youth

Tina Byrom and Sheine Peart

 is an imprint of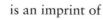

Trentham Books

IOE Press

First published in 2017 by the UCL Institute of Education Press, University College London, 20 Bedford Way, London WC1H 0AL

www.ucl-ioe-press.com

© Tina Byrom and Sheine Peart 2017

British Library Cataloguing in Publication Data:
A catalogue record for this publication is available from the British Library

ISBNs
978-1-85856-804-1 (paperback)
978-1-85856-828-7 (PDF eBook)
978-1-85856-829-4 (ePub eBook)
978-1-85856-830-0 (Kindle eBook)

Every effort has been made to trace copyright holders and to obtain their permission for the use of copyright material. The publisher apologizes for any errors or omissions and would be grateful if notified of any corrections that should be incorporated in future reprints or editions of this book.

The opinions expressed in this publication are those of the author and do not necessarily reflect the views of University College London.

Typeset by Quadrant Infotech (India) Pvt Ltd
Printed by CPI Group (UK) Ltd, Croydon, CR0 4YY

Cover image © Andrew Parker/Alamy Stock Photo

Contents

List of figures and tables

Acknowledgements

The authors are sincerely grateful to everyone who has contributed to the production of this book. There are too many to name individually (but you know who you are!).

Particular thanks go to the young people who opened up to us during interview. We were privileged to enter into their worlds as they shared their experiences through telling their stories.

We would also like to thank all Housing Association staff who supported the young people and candidly provided extra information that contextualized the individuals in their support programme. It is clear to us that without the interventions provided by the Nottingham Community Housing Association the lives of the young people featured in this book would be very different.

We are extremely grateful to Professor Penny Burke for providing her insights into marginalized groups and for taking time out of her busy schedule to write the foreword for us.

And last but by no means least, we are truly thankful to Gillian Klein for her enduring patience and belief that we would get the book completed.

About the authors

Dr Tina Byrom is an established academic, with over 25 years' teaching experience across compulsory, post-compulsory and higher education. She works as a Consultant Researcher after recently leaving senior management at Nottingham Trent University. Tina's research focuses on social justice and she has published in the field of transition, widening participation and non-traditional learners. She completed her PhD thesis, 'The Dream of Social Flying': Social Class, Higher Education Choice and the Paradox of Widening Participation', at the University of Nottingham in 2008 and presents at national and international conferences as a result of this research. The numerous research projects she has worked on include Understanding Teenage Pregnancy in Nottingham, Health Imperatives in Schools, HE Participation Rates in Nottingham North, and FE Provision in Nottingham City.

Dr Sheine Peart has worked in education for over 30 years in schools, colleges, local authorities, further education, higher education and youth and community settings and has a lifetime passion for working on equalities issues. She was the manager for 15 years of teacher education courses in FE. She led a team dedicated to raising the achievement of African Caribbean pupils and was an equalities manager. Currently manager of the PhD Education course at Nottingham Trent University, she works with students who are completing their doctorates and also contributes to Master's and undergraduate courses. Her book *Making Education Work* (2013) shines a light on how effective further educational provision was for Black boys compared with the school sector's. Sheine has guest-edited an edition of the journal *Race Equality Teaching*.

Foreword

This important book reveals and analyses an aspect of social inequality often invisible and under-researched as well as under-theorized. The experiences of youth homelessness are rarely explored and are often only known through decontextualized and disembodied data that tells us something about the numbers of young people who are homeless. What is silenced are the young people's voices, their stories and the contexts and social dynamics in which they are placed in such vulnerable, marginalizing and dangerous situations. The representation of young people's voices in this book brings to life the complex issues surrounding experiences of homelessness and how these are compounded by a range of interconnected policy and social dynamics, as well as changing family structures. This is done sensitively by Tina Byrom and Sheine Peart, crafted by their careful, critical and reflexive attention to questions of power, ethics, representation and voice. The emotional and affective dimensions shaping the young people's experiences are explored, with themes of alienation, loneliness, fear and loss as well as aspiration, desire and hope.

Much of the contemporary discourses that shape how we imagine social problems such as homelessness construct and oversimplify the issue as an individual one. Our increasingly marketized and neoliberalized society often misrepresents young people and their families as making free choices and decisions that result either in 'success' or 'failure'. The structures, systems, policies and practices that often exacerbate positions of marginality and vulnerability are concealed, while pathologizing narratives distort our understanding and shape our flawed assumptions. Thus youth homelessness is often regarded as an individual problem, making it easier for us to turn away, to dismiss the issue as the fault of the young person suffering it, rather than to engage in deeper understanding about the multiple and underlying social and cultural factors that contribute to the significant levels of vulnerability many are forced to face so early in their lives. The interconnecting issues that might come together to manifest in homelessness create a situation in which young people's participation in employment, education and training is severely impeded. A vicious and toxic cycle of social exclusion and poverty is put into place.

The book brings to light the crucial point that when such complex issues are reduced to individualism, the opportunity is lost for deeper levels of understanding that can lead to transformative policies and practices.

Thus it is important to draw on critical theories that illuminate the complex processes by which homelessness is made possible. This means we must understand the issue in all its multifaceted dimensions and not seek simple, quick-fix answers that end up exacerbating vicious cycles. In my own work, I have drawn from an eclectic set of conceptual tools to contribute to deepening understanding of social exclusion and marginalization, particularly in relation to access to education and learning (Burke, 2012). Nancy Fraser's multidimensional approach to social justice of redistribution, recognition and representation (1997, 2003, 2005) makes a vital contribution to challenging individualizing discourses that perpetuate flawed and impoverished explanations. Such discourses 'misframe' the problem – and it is clear from this important book that youth homelessness is too often misframed, which then exacerbates the vulnerability of already vulnerable young people whose experiences are misrepresented and whose bodies are misrecognized. Fraser's framework helps us to understand that in order to address social issues such as youth homelessness, we need a range of strategies that redistribute resources, provide access to opportunities and develop knowledge for those young people facing social exclusion. We need to understand, value and recognize their aspirations, experiences and stories through enabling their full representation in processes of decision-making and social change and through facilitating access to high-quality education and employment.

There are a number of other important conceptual tools to draw on in such a social justice reorientation to tackle the problem of youth homelessness. For example, feminist perspectives help to bring to focus the gendered nature of vulnerability in relation to gendered violence and abuse and the problematic construction of hegemonic masculinity, femininity and sexuality in contemporary societies. Conceptual tools that draw on poststructural theories help bring to light the complex nature of power. An understanding of power as fluid, dynamic, shifting and generative helps us to develop critical, reflexive and collective strategies to counter social inequalities. This requires representation of a range of different voices and experiences including of the young people themselves, as well as careful listening. The young people's accounts included in this book demonstrate their tenacity, resilience and hope; the individual strengths that must be valued and recognized, and then built upon by high-quality support mechanisms, such as the housing association and peer mentoring programmes outlined by the authors.

We need to reframe the issue of youth homelessness through the lens of social justice; and we must challenge those pathologizing explanations that blame the individual for what are social problems. Simultaneously, we need to redistribute opportunities to individuals to support the development of their capacity.

Penny Jane Burke
Global Innovation Chair of Equity
University of Newcastle, Australia

Chapter 1

Closing inn: What's the problem?

Introduction

The need for a secure base is a fundamental human one. While housing and homes are influenced by prevailing cultural norms, and differ according to economic and global positioning, most societies are organized so that their citizens live somewhere they can call home. Although this accommodation might only be temporary, and the transient nature of the housing is known to the residents, it still provides a base from which individuals can organize other aspects of their lives and a place they can return to to rest. Homes act as a physical and emotional anchor, tying individuals to a location and enabling them to put down roots and form community links. Homes provide a redoubt where people can recover from their travails, a refuge and sanctuary, or, as the adage proclaims, 'a man's home is his castle'.

As early as 1943 Maslow identified shelter as one of the elementary safety needs of all people, an idea further developed by the United Nations Universal Declaration of Human Rights (1948), which, echoing the old proverb, states, 'Everyone has the right to own property alone as well as in association with others. No one shall be arbitrarily deprived of his property' (United Nations, 1948: Article 17). A contemporary social justice agenda, which recognizes all citizens as valued members, demands that society provides everyone with equal social rights, including access to decent housing. The present study, which originated in the evaluation of one housing project's services, explored whether the project, in addition to providing a safe home, gave the support needed to help young people become active agents in controlling the direction of their lives and helped them to develop the skills, knowledge and capabilities required to steer the direction of their futures.

A number of themes recur throughout this book: the ongoing impact of education, family and personal relationships, agency and individual resilience, aspirations for the future, and access to appropriate support mechanisms, including housing projects. To provide an additional dimension to this study, other related themes of health and employment opportunities are explored and integrated throughout the chapters.

For the purposes of this study, a 'young person' is anyone between 14 and 25 years old.

The opening chapter of this book begins the discussion of youth homelessness by examining the complexities of this problem and reviewing some of the typical challenges faced by homeless young people. Chapter 2 extends the discussion of homelessness by providing a national and global perspective on youth homelessness and exploring the (in)action of governments to address this issue. Chapter 3 investigates some of the support mechanisms available to young people once they become homeless and considers an innovative government-supported initiative for managing the problem of youth homelessness. The background to this research project is explored in Chapter 4, which provides details of the approaches used to help the young people open up and provide a candid account of their life experiences. Chapters 5 to 9 are the personal narratives of the young people who took part in this project, describing their past disappointments and their hopes for a better life in the future. Chapter 10 considers the ways in which one housing project based in the Midlands was helping young people manage their immediate problems and providing them with the support needed for their futures. Chapter 11 looks at the personal and cross-agency actions needed to end youth homelessness, and the final chapter summarizes the problem of youth homelessness and its demoralizing impact on young people, but also identifies potential positive interventions.

Youth homelessness: what's the problem?

Youth homelessness is a global problem. In the United States alone there are 'approximately 1.7 million' reported homeless young people (Tevendale *et al.*, 2011: 615); in Dublin, Ireland, the number of homeless children and their families 'increased by approximately 15 per cent' from 1999 to 2002 (Keogh *et al.*, 2006: 361); another study estimated there were 'between 10,000 and 20,000 homeless young people in the Netherlands between the ages of 16 and 21' (Van der Ploeg, 1989: 50). The UK has similar problems, and in 2014 '[n]early half of people living in homeless accommodation services' were under 24 (Homeless Link, 2015: 3). In 2015, while only '16,000 young people were officially classed as "statutory homeless"' (Owen, 2015), over '136,000 young people aged between 16 and 24 in England and Wales sought emergency housing' (ibid.) and 'the number of households living in temporary accommodation peaked at the end of September 2004 … [t]he number has been gradually rising since 2012' (DCLG, 2015b: 1). Youth homelessness is not going away and at the moment the situation is steadily worsening.

Despite being 'one of the most vulnerable groups in society' (Homeless Link, 2015: 6), after becoming homeless young people often struggle to find accommodation even though they are defined as a statutory priority group. Their youth is perceived as an advantage, a source of strength which provides the robustness needed to accommodate setbacks. However, homelessness exposes young people to a number of challenging situations at a time in their lives when they have neither the skills nor the knowledge needed to manage these difficulties. Consequently, rather than enhancing resilience, their youth puts them in greater danger of being exploited or developing other problems, and they may struggle with alcohol and substance misuse, mental and physical health problems, and unemployment and its consequent financial issues. Accordingly, many homeless young people are 'under a lot more stress than the average kid ... and they tend to be more sickly' (Robertson, 2006: 160). Without appropriate adult guidance, 'many of these kids raise themselves' (ibid.). These problems are frequently compounded by an inability to form the kind of positive social networks which could help them manage their troubles, and they may become loners, for fear of becoming 'attached and having to move again' (ibid.).

Because they lack a safe, secure base and reliable, consistent adult guidance, homeless young people are easy prey to older adults who are routinely engaged in a variety of criminal activities, such as drug misuse and supply, theft or handling stolen goods. Homeless youths may even become actively involved in crime themselves, graduating from lesser roles, such as being a lookout or a depository for goods, to organizing and committing the principal crime. Research completed by Crisis has shown that '34% [of young homeless people] have committed a minor crime, such as shoplifting' (2012: 6), crimes which some homeless people believe are necessary if they are to survive. Even without taking part in offences, the very act of being homeless is a criminal offence; the 1824 Vagrancy Act states that 'wandering abroad ... and not giving a good account of himself or herself' (legislation. gov.uk, 2017) merits arrest. As recently as 2008 over 1800 people were prosecuted under this Act, and it appears that 'the British government and urban managers have adopted an increasingly aggressive stance towards street homeless people' (Johnsen *et al.*, 2005: 788) and 'a number of cities across the USA, Canada and Britain [are] now deploying a range of punitive measures designed to control and contain homeless people' (ibid.). While the Vagrancy Act remains on the statute, simply being homeless can result in gaining a criminal record, and at present there is no indication that this Act will be repealed.

As well as the inherent problems of vulnerability and potential involvement in crime, lacking stable accommodation creates further difficulties in relation to education, health and employment. Without appropriate support from the agencies dealing with these three vital areas the needs of homeless youths exponentially increase and they are exposed to more hazards and even bigger risks. Simply put, the needs of homeless youth are far greater, rather than less, than those of young people who live in safe, settled accommodation where they can rely on suitable support from adults who care about their emotional, physical and financial health.

Educational challenges for homeless youth

There is an intrinsic, complex relationship between education and homelessness. Although going to school or college is 'an everyday component of most children's lives, [it] is typically fraught with difficulties' (Walsh, 1992: 6) for homeless young people. Education is recognized as one of the bedrocks of contemporary society. It not only provides the skills and knowledge seen as important for employment and economic prosperity, in many ways it also represents an extension of the family base, responsible for introducing and reinforcing expected standards of behaviour and morality. In addition, education enables young people to form networks beyond their immediate family and to understand fitting behaviour in a variety of social and work-related contexts. However, homeless young people miss many of these opportunities by not accessing education at all or by having broken education journeys.

For young people aged 14–16 access to full-time state education depends on accommodation stability. Local authorities assume young people, as minors, will be living at home with their families. Consequently authorities routinely contact parents or guardians (not the young people themselves) to advise them of school admission procedures and locally available places. To set up a secondary school place, local authority contact would normally occur towards the end of primary school. If a young person becomes homeless after leaving primary school, or moves area, they may lose an existing secondary school place. If the young person is not living with a family or under local authority care at a permanent address, they will not be advised of space in a new school, not least because local authorities may have no reliable point of contact. While local authorities have a statutory duty to help 14–16-year-olds gain accommodation and a legal obligation to enforce their schooling, 'over half [the young homeless people surveyed] found the support they were offered was not helpful' (Crisis, 2012: 3). Worse still, many were 'simply turned away' (ibid.) and given no guidance on how to obtain housing or schooling. For those unfamiliar with an area the situation may be even harder as they may not know who to contact or where council offices are located. Even when young people are able to secure accommodation, residence alone does not guarantee a school place; some may go to their nearest school expecting to be enrolled, only to be refused admission or advised that they need to make a formal application to attend.

Young people aged 16 and over can apply to a sixth-form or FE college, most of which operate a direct applications procedure. However, applicants are usually asked for a fixed address, and applicants aged 16–18, still being minors, may be asked if their parents or guardians consent to the application. Some application forms also require a parent's or guardian's signature, which is difficult for young people who are estranged from their families. While most colleges are willing to help students complete application forms, these three requirements (fixed address, consent and signature) are unhelpful obstacles for homeless youth trying to access education and may deter some young people from applying.

Transferring schools is a stressful time for young people because it involves moving from familiar surroundings, where locations and organizational demands are understood, to another environment where everything is new. School transfer is a big decision and one more often necessitated by circumstances than taken by free choice. Local authorities encourage families to keep secondary school students in the same school if at all possible, to avoid them having to undergo the disruption changing schools involves. If circumstances dictate that a change of school is inevitable, many families invest considerable time and energy in preparing young people for their new school by explaining what the young person can expect on arrival and what the school will require. This might include arranging visits or attending orientation days where newcomers are shown the facilities, meet staff and are told about systems and structures. Welcome days like this usually happen in September and are designed to facilitate a smooth transfer. However, becoming homeless does not adhere to a specific timetable and young people may need to transfer schools outside standard admission times. Some schools provide individual bespoke orientations for individual students, but they are not obliged to do so. Moving schools and not taking part in reception events may heighten a young person's stress levels and make entering the new environment more challenging.

Even when young people successfully secure a school place, they are not guaranteed a socially or educationally smooth transition. As a result of being homeless young people may have lost the routine disciplines required by most schools; they may struggle with punctuality, find it hard to conform to expected norms, lack sufficient funds to buy apparatus or take part in educational activities, or be without the right uniform. To try and support students who struggle to buy the correct clothing or apparatus, some schools offer used uniforms free or at a discount price and keep a collection of second-hand equipment. However, collectively these differences combine to make the young person more conspicuous and less able to make a seamless, straightforward transition. Their dissimilarity identifies them as a stranger, hindering both social and academic integration and making them a potential target. Furthermore, simply being new puts them at risk of being seen as an outsider, as friendship groups are quickly established and can be resistant to admitting others. Students may also struggle with academic transition. They may not have taken relevant assessments and may be allocated to academically inappropriate classes, sets or streams. As a result of thorny academic and social integration, many find school life difficult: 'over half (51%) of young homeless people have been suspended or excluded from school' (Crisis, 2012: 4).

Success in education depends on progression inside and outside school and requires skills application and knowledge development beyond the classroom. However, being in transit makes it difficult to participate in school life on both these levels. Accommodation allocated to homeless people, especially temporary housing, is commonly minimal and may lack suitable space to complete assignments. Failure to complete homework can result in 'falling behind' (Powney, 2001: 369) and academic underachievement. Consequently, some young people cannot see the relevance of education, while others come to hate formal learning. These circumstances combine to produce a cruel sequence of successive disappointments, where being homeless makes it difficult to persevere with education, not persisting makes it difficult to succeed academically, and not succeeding limits future employment opportunities and thus increases the likelihood of continued homelessness.

Health challenges for homeless youth

Being homeless produces a 'range of detrimental effects on ... well-being' (Powney, 2001: 368). Young homeless people have a higher incidence of health care needs than their settled contemporaries: '41% have mental health problems and 30% sometimes self harm. Around a third are dependent on alcohol and almost 40% dependent on drugs' (Crisis, 2012: 4); many engage in 'high risk sexual behaviors' (Nebbitt *et al.*, 2007: 550); and 'inadequate facilities in emergency accommodation, such as overcrowding, can aggravate health problems' (Keogh *et al.*, 2006: 366). In addition, many homeless people have unhealthy lifestyles, which

> can cause long-term health problems or exacerbate existing issues. Analysis of the latest data found that 77% of homeless people smoke, 35% do not eat at least two meals a day and two-thirds consume more than the recommended amount of alcohol each time they drink.
>
> (Homeless Link, 2014a: 3)

Smoking, poor diet and excessive alcohol consumption not only cause illness but also contribute to lowered immunity. Consequently, many homeless people live in a constant state of poor health and there are far higher rates of premature death (ibid.: 5) in the homeless population.

Access to appropriate health care has long been a problem for homeless youth (Walsh, 1992: 6), and *remains one today*. Health care, like education, is linked to living in sustained accommodation. However, it is a myth that individuals need a permanent address to register with a GP; 'anyone who doesn't have a home address can legitimately register by using the surgery's address instead' (Crisis, n.d.: [3]). Unfortunately not all GP surgeries are aware of this information; 'Many surgeries mistakenly think that homeless people need to have an address in order to register' (ibid.). Some homeless people have even reported being 'turned away from medical practices because they didn't have one' (ibid.).

Because many homeless people are not registered with a GP and there are few drop-in services available, they make disproportionate use of emergency health provision. Recent research by Homeless Link reported that 'the number of A&E visits and hospital admissions per homeless person [is] four times higher than for the general public' (2014a: 11). This costs the health service '£85m per year' (ibid.) and places significant strain on available resources. Further, emergency services are usually only able to provide short-term, critical care. However, '[m]any homeless people suffer from a debilitating combination of mental health, addiction and physical health problems … [and] some of them had lived with the same complex mixture of problems' for a considerable time (Crisis, n.d.: [3]). Acute health services cannot easily cater for the chronic, persistent or complex conditions, such as respiratory illnesses, mania or psychosis, which are prevalent among homeless people. Homeless people's health is placed at further risk because their health needs may not be adequately monitored or there may be a break in care as they move addresses. As a result the health care needs of many homeless young people receive only minimal attention, are undiagnosed or do not receive an appropriate level of sustained attention.

In summary, while being homeless is not the sole cause of ill health, it is a major contributory factor in the continued poor health of many homeless people. Although 'statutory services have a duty to ensure … young people at risk remain safe from harm, not all authorities have resources to provide a service appropriate to [their] complex needs' (Franks *et al.*, 2015: 149) and a 'significant number of homeless people report that they are not receiving help with their health care problems' (Homeless Link, 2014a: 3). Consequently, many young homeless people have poor physical and mental health, conditions which often become worse.

Employment challenges for homeless youth

Employment is the route to both independent living and securing accommodation; there is an inherent link between sustained employment and having a home base. However, finding and keeping a job is a considerable challenge for homeless young people, many of whom have had interrupted or unsuccessful education histories and lack sufficient or relevant qualifications to find employment. Research by Crisis found that 'just over one third (37 per cent) of homeless people do not have any formal qualifications' (Opinion Leader Research, 2006: 3), which further limited their options in respect of potential employment. Another barrier to finding employment is that some prospective 'employers require a permanent address' (ibid.: 26), and there is an implied assumption of greater reliability in young people in secure accommodation.

Being homeless can also contribute to an erosion of the skills and attributes needed to find and retain employment. Preparing for a day's work becomes more challenging without somewhere to take a shower or a place to store and retrieve clean work clothes. The routines needed for employment, such as arriving at work at the correct time, while possible, are not easily supported without fixed housing. As a consequence, while 'the vast majority of homeless people want to work' (Crisis, 2014), many struggle to find employment.

In addition to requiring common skills and attitudes (summarized in Table 1.1) some employers are reluctant to invest in staff training and wish employees to arrive 'work-ready'. Homeless youth can find themselves in a '"Catch-22" situation where employers want relevant experience[;] however[,] they are unable to get experience until they get a job' (Crisis,

2006: 26). While being homeless does not automatically mean young people will lack skills, being homeless limits the opportunities to develop many work-focused competencies. For example, although the itinerant nature of being in 'no fixed abode' may provide (impose) opportunities to use initiative and improvise, it will probably not support the opportunity to develop team-working skills, and not having a permanent base may result in less attention to personal hygiene.

Table 1.1 General employment skills needed

Organizational skills	Interpersonal skills	Attitudes
Dresses appropriately for role	Good team working skills	Positive attitude
Attends with correct equipment	Co-operative nature	Pleasant disposition
Good time keeping	Uses language appropriately	Honest
Ability to keep to schedules	Good personal hygiene	Respectful of hierarchies
	Respectful to other colleagues	Reliable
	Ability to use initiative	Responsible
		Willingness to learn

Source: Peart and Atkins (2011: 70). Reproduced by kind permission of Sage Publishing.

This situation is compounded by the changing expectations of employers, and '[i]n the economy of the 21st Century, higher education is required for most professional jobs .... For those with a high school degree or less, the unemployment rate is high, and incomes are poor' (Gwadz *et al.*, 2009: 358). Most homeless people lack higher-level qualifications and only just over 'one in ten (13 per cent) homeless people have Level Three qualifications or above .... This is less than a third of the national average of 46 per cent of the adult population' (Crisis, 2006: 11). Homeless people therefore find themselves in a cycle of limited employment opportunities.

With few positive options, some homeless young people enter a street-based economy that includes 'itinerant informal work (housecleaning, ..., manual labor, etc.), as well as sex work (also referred to as commercial or survival sex) shoplifting, selling stolen goods, mugging, and activities of the illegal drug economy' (Gwadz *et al.*, 2009: 358). Some of these activities increase the likelihood of homeless people being arrested and gaining a criminal record, which, once acquired, negatively influences the opportunities to gain employment.

Conclusion

Youth homelessness is complex. While some young people become homeless because of a single catastrophic incident, for others homelessness is the culmination of events which have occurred over time. Though each incident in itself need not necessarily result in homelessness, unless appropriate support is provided in a timely way, such events can escalate and end in a young person leaving or being ejected from their home. Although family break-up remains the most common cause of youth homelessness other factors, such as changes in the benefits system and overcrowding, have put further pressure on families' ability to cope, thus contributing to the rise in youth homelessness. While most local authorities are aware of the scale and scope of the problem and are committed to supporting young people in their efforts to gain secure accommodation, it is a concern that 'local authorities continue to report they do not have an adequate range of tools to address homelessness prevention' (Homeless Link, 2015: 40).

Youth homelessness does not just happen. It is a problem that has built up over time through many stages. In the same way, youth homelessness will not be solved by a universal panacea. To address this problem there will need to be a concerted multi-agency approach from national and local government (including education, health and employment services), voluntary sector groups and charitable organizations, with an emphasis on early intervention to prevent homelessness from occurring. Critically, support programmes to enable young people to make informed decisions need to be developed so that they can become active agents in their future biographies.

Chapter 2

Contextual view of homelessness in the UK

Introduction

Drawing from official reports and literature, this chapter provides an overview of the levels of homelessness in the UK. It illuminates the contradictory information that different agencies involved with homelessness provide and exposes how the rhetoric emanating from government offices is far removed from the heart of the problem. Attention is drawn to the particular features of youth homelessness and the challenges faced by this group in repairing the damage that has been caused through their repeated and sustained disadvantages in fractured communities.

The national picture of homelessness is explored through an examination of the political and economic climate. It highlights the low priority afforded to homelessness by successive governments. This was particularly evident from the attention paid to protestors camped at St Paul's Cathedral and the resultant outcry against those prepared to take a firm stance in demanding social equality.

Different definitions of homelessness

Homeless young people are representative of a perceived 'lost generation' (Bell and Blanchflower, 2010: 17). While homelessness is viewed as a social and political issue, it is often a manifestation of a range of interconnected issues, including mental health issues, disadvantage, unemployment, and low levels of education. Of specific concern are the 'particularly strong evidence that homelessness impedes young people's participation in employment, education or training' (Quilgars *et al.*, 2008: 2) and the claim that European countries have broken their 'social contract' (OECD, 2011, quoting OECD Secretary-General Ángel Gurría) with young people as a result. However, despite this bleak picture, there are a range of services that seek to bring about change in the lives of young people who, for one reason or another, find themselves homeless. Such services tend to focus on preventative measures or interventions (supporting the young person back to education to improve life chances).

Homelessness is a broad term that has numerous interpretations (DCLG, 2016c). Importantly, and pertinent to this study, is the inclusion of those living in shelters, living in temporary accommodation, 'sofa surfing' with friends or relatives or living in squats (Bachu, 2016). Thus, sleeping rough on the streets is only one element of a broader definition of homelessness.

Shelter (2016), the housing and homeless charity, provides a definition that goes beyond that detailed in government documentation. It identifies the complexity of homelessness by drawing attention to the factors that combine to make life difficult for particular groups of people:

> If you have a home, you could be considered homeless if you live
> in very overcrowded conditions or in poor conditions that affect
> your health or you're at risk of violence or abuse in your home.
>
> (Shelter, 2016)

They also suggest that people may be considered to be homeless if they:

- live somewhere where they have no legal right to stay, such as a squat
- live in a home they can't afford to pay for without depriving themselves of basic essentials
- are forced to live apart from their family or someone they would normally live with because their accommodation isn't suitable.

People who fall into such categories and definitions of homelessness clearly face a range of challenges, depending on the reason for their homelessness in the first place. For the young people in this study, the initial cause of their homelessness was invariably dysfunctional family backgrounds. This will be explored in more detail in Chapter 6.

The problem with homelessness research

Kennedy and Fitzpatrick (2001) identify numerous problems with research on the issue of homelessness. First, they argue that much of the research is 'descriptive and a-theoretical' (p. 2003). They also identify the ways in which explanations tend to focus on either structural causes or individual pathology as a way of understanding the problem:

> The explanations which do exist of homelessness tend to
> emphasise either structural causes (changes to the benefits
> system and a shortage of social housing) or individual pathology
> (resulting from the 'choice' or 'vulnerability' of certain 'types'

of people), although some accounts have attempted to weave together consideration of both micro- and macro-level factors.

(Kennedy and Fitzpatrick, 2001: 2003)

Importantly, they argue, 'polarised explanations' (ibid.) are unable to account for why people become homeless. In fact, it has been acknowledged that identifying the causation of homelessness is complex:

> Theoretical, historical and international perspectives all indicate that the causation of homelessness is complex, with no single 'trigger' that is either 'necessary' or 'sufficient' for it to occur. Individual, interpersonal and structural factors all play a role – and interact with each other – and the balance of causes differs over time, across countries, and between demographic groups.
>
> (Fitzpatrick *et al.*, 2012: x)

Irrespective of the issues identified in the theoretical explanations of homelessness, there is a concomitant layer of complexity in the process of being identified as homeless. This is a key issue, because being categorized as homeless is not in itself sufficient to enable people to access any local authority support. The difficulties this poses has some influence on the perpetuation of social exclusion for a large number of people. In order to qualify for support or intervention, homeless people need to be categorized as statutorily homeless.

Statutory homelessness

In order to access the support of local authority interventions, young people need to be recognized as homeless. To be statutorily homeless, they are required to meet specific legislative criteria, namely Part 7 of the Housing Act 1996 as amended by the Homelessness Act 2002, and the Localism Act 2011, which provides the principal statutory framework for homelessness legislation in England. Once people or households are recognized by their local authority as homeless, they are included in official government homelessness statistics. It is essential for young people, or anyone facing homelessness, to achieve official recognition of their homelessness if they are to access the full range of support available. Broadly, a person is 'homeless' if they are not legally entitled to occupy accommodation that is accessible, physically available to them (and their household) and reasonably fit to live in.

In England, local authorities have legal duties to homeless people. However, there are criteria which a homeless person must meet in order to qualify as statutorily homeless, which will trigger local authority intervention. A local authority will consider the applicant's eligibility and what, if any, intervention should be provided. The 'main homelessness duty' – to secure suitable settled accommodation – is owed to those who are 'not intentionally' homeless and fall within a priority need group. Shelter (2014) alerts us to the following:

> If a council decides that you are legally homeless or threatened with homelessness, it may eventually have to help you by providing you with settled accommodation. If it decides you are not homeless, you don't get the same level of help.
>
> (Shelter, 2014)

Access to local authority support is considered on the basis of priority, or, as Neale (1997: 47) suggests, based on a process that has 'frequently classified [homeless people] as either deserving or undeserving'. From a government perspective, priority need groups include households with dependent children or a pregnant woman, and individuals who are vulnerable in some way. In order to be classified as vulnerable, an individual will:

- have mental illness or physical disability
- be a young person (16 to 17 years old, or 18 to 20 years old and vulnerable as a result of previously being in care)
- be vulnerable as a result of previously being in custody
- be vulnerable as a result of previously being in HM Forces, or
- be forced to flee their home because of violence or the threat of violence.

This list provides some insight into the challenges faced by those who experience homelessness and are in need of local authority intervention. However, individuals may experience homelessness but not fall into the 'statutory' homelessness category. Non-statutory homelessness applies to individuals who are not owed the main homelessness duty because they do not come into a priority need category. In these cases, the local authority only has a duty to provide advice and assistance. Such people are frequently referred to as 'the single homeless'. In 2015, 19,540 households applied to local authorities for support but were not considered as being in priority need (DCLG, 2016a: Table 770).

The process of being categorized as homeless hides the true scale of the homelessness problem. Crisis (2016a) highlights the 'hidden homelessness', which includes people who do not qualify for local authority housing assistance and may be staying in a hostel, with friends or in some other form of temporary and insecure accommodation. Hostels and other forms of temporary accommodation for homeless people are recorded only via a set of incomplete and overlapping data sets; there is no official register of temporary accommodation or its occupants, which makes it difficult to determine the total number of people in this type of accommodation. Outside even such temporary or insecure accommodation is a range of individuals who would not feature in official homelessness data: rough sleepers and the street-dwelling homeless.

Rough sleeping

Kennedy and Fitzpatrick (2001: 2001) define rough sleeping as sleeping 'in the open air or in a place not designed for habitation for at least one night'. This view is also seen in the Department for Communities and Local Government's definition, which includes the following people in the count figure of rough sleepers:

> People sleeping, about to bed down (sitting on/in or standing next to their bedding) or actually bedded down in the open air (such as on the streets, in tents, doorways, parks, bus shelters or encampments). People in buildings or other places not designed for habitation (such as stairwells, barns, sheds, car parks, cars, derelict boats, stations, or 'bashes').
>
> (DCLG, 2010: 6)

Rough sleeping is one indicator of a range of difficulties experienced by people who find themselves homeless. Pleace (2000: 581) acknowledges this by stating:

> The dominant paradigm suggests that people sleeping rough are often individuals who are predisposed to becoming homeless because their individual characteristics make them especially vulnerable to changes in housing supply, labour markets and other structural factors that precipitate homelessness.

The picture presented here is one that is indicative of multiple forms of disadvantage that tend to lend themselves to increased vulnerability to increased difficulties, one of which is homelessness. Recent figures suggest that there has been an increase in the numbers of rough sleepers despite the strategies that had seen some success as a result of Labour Government policies:

> By the end of the Labour Government's period in office, in 2010, there had been some notable achievements on homelessness. In

particular, there had been a sustained large reduction in levels of recorded rough sleeping, and an unprecedented decline in statutory homelessness from 2003, associated with a step-change in Ministerial priority accorded to homelessness prevention.

(Fitzpatrick *et al.*, 2012: xi)

However, it is impossible to gain a full picture of the numbers of rough sleepers, as official data is pulled together from counts or estimates provided by local authorities. The method for ascertaining the numbers of rough sleepers has received much criticism (see ibid.: 63) on the grounds that:

- snapshot counts are misleading as they cannot be wholly comprehensive
- snapshot counts distort the scale of the problem as they cannot account for duration of homelessness
- the level of resources for snapshot counts is inadequate
- the procedure for summing the total number of rough sleepers is flawed.

Therefore, snapshot counts inevitably underestimate the numbers of those affected by homelessness over a given time period (Fitzpatrick *et al.*, 2012). In addition, the different demographic groups affected by homelessness are difficult to fully ascertain through existing enumeration methods. Despite this, while it has been acknowledged that there were some improvements to rough sleeping during the Labour Government period, the same was not true for some demographic groups, including refugees. In addition,

[m]ost single homeless people remained without the statutory safety net in England, and had no legal rights to even emergency accommodation when roofless unless in a 'priority need group' (in this sense the *legal* safety net for rough sleepers in England remained weaker than that in a number of other European countries).

(ibid.: xi)

Rough sleepers could therefore access the appropriate level of local authority intervention provided they met one of the priority criteria listed on p. 14 above. While the numbers of rough sleepers is difficult to determine, and there were some improvements during the Labour Government, the picture deteriorated to some extent under the Coalition Government. The 2015 Homelessness Monitor Report recognizes that homelessness figures continued to increase as a result of government policies (Fitzpatrick *et al.*, 2015). The 2016 report identifies a particular need for temporary accommodation, which showed a 12% increase on the previous year. The report clearly lays the blame at the door of the Government, stating:

> More and more people are struggling to keep a roof over their heads, and as this report warns, recent housing and welfare changes could make it even harder for low income households to find a place to live.
>
> (Sparkes and Unwin, 2016: vi)

This report also highlights the issues inherent in gaining an accurate picture of statutory homelessness across the UK. This is particularly the case for statutorily homeless individuals who are categorized as part of the 'hidden homeless'. One such group that causes concern is the street homeless, as it is impossible to account for all individuals who sleep on the streets.

Street homelessness

Street homelessness is a much wider term than rough sleeping, taking into account the street lifestyles of some people who may not actually sleep on the streets. Street homeless people are those who routinely find themselves on the streets during the day with nowhere to go at night. Some will end up sleeping outside, or in a derelict or other building not designed for human habitation, perhaps for long periods. Others will sleep at a friend's for a very short time, or stay in a hostel, night-shelter or squat, or spend nights in prison or hospital (Diaz, 2006).

Street homelessness has been a policy priority in the UK for some time, with successive governments investing substantial resources in attempts to reduce its prevalence. In England, recent years have witnessed the increasing use of 'control' as well as 'care' in various initiatives targeting rough sleepers and those involved in 'problematic street culture' such as begging and street drinking (Johnsen *et al.*, 2016).

Given the instability of the homeless population, the national picture is somewhat difficult to determine. However, the next section deals with the national picture as determined by official statistics.

Homelessness national data

Measuring the incidence of homelessness is anything but straightforward. A large part of the problem is the imprecise nature of the term and the different ways in which it is used to designate degrees of homelessness. Despite the issues inherent in capturing accurate homelessness data, research shows that policy direction, in particular welfare cuts, is likely to contribute to a sustained increase in homelessness:

We continue to see a sustained increase in levels of homelessness in England due to the ongoing economic downturn combined with the initial impact of weakening welfare protections, especially housing benefit. This report is clear that in 2012 we have not yet seen the full impact of welfare reforms and that the coming year is likely to see a much more dramatic increase in homelessness as transitional protections are ended and further cuts come into force.

(Morphy, 2012: vii)

The Department for Communities and Local Government (DCLG, 2016a: Table 784) recorded that in 2015–16 57,730 people in England were accepted as homeless by their local authority under the 1996 Housing Act. This means they were deemed unintentionally homeless and 'in priority need' and therefore eligible for local authority intervention. This figure represents a 6% increase on the 2014–15 figure, when 54,430 people were accepted as homeless. Existing studies that monitor rates of homelessness acknowledge that the figures cannot accurately indicate actual figures of homelessness (see, for example, Fitzpatrick *et al.*, 2016).

Government street counts and estimates give a snapshot of the national situation in relation to rough sleeping. In 2015 they estimated around 3,569 people sleep rough on any one night across England. This is an increase of 30% on the 2014 figure of 2,744 and is more than double the number in autumn 2010, when the figure was 1,768 (DCLG, 2016b). As already addressed above, the rise in the number of homeless has been linked to changes in government policy.

The demographic group that faces a disproportionate risk of homelessness is young people (see, for example, Quilgars *et al.*, 2008; Watts *et al.*, 2015). Young people are generally understood to be between the ages of 16 and 24 unless otherwise specified. The next section turns to this particular demographic group, as it is the group most pertinent to this study.

Homeless young people nationally

Supporting homeless young people is a particularly acute problem, with nine out of ten councils reporting that they find it difficult to support those aged 16–24 (Fitzpatrick *et al.*, 2016). Young people become homeless because of a range of issues with family life. Those most at risk of becoming homeless experience high levels of disadvantage, along with other forms of childhood disruption. As Quilgars *et al.* (2008: xii) note:

[y]oung people who have experienced disruption or trauma during childhood and/or who are from poor socio-economic backgrounds are at increased risk of homelessness. The main 'trigger' for homelessness among young people is relationship breakdown (usually with parents or step-parents). For many, this is a consequence of long-term conflict within the home and often involves violence.

Young homeless people are considered to be considerably more vulnerable than the overall homeless population. For example, 51% have been excluded from school, 40% have experienced abuse at home and 33% self-harm (Crisis, 2012). In addition, of the total number of households accepted as homeless during 2015–16, the main applicant in 23% of them was aged 16–24. This percentage equates to 13,280 young people (DCLG, 2016a: Table 781).

As with all forms of homelessness, obtaining an accurate measure of the young homeless is problematic. Official homelessness statistics only record the number of 'priority need' young people local authorities have a statutory duty to house, such as young parents or under-18s. Centrepoint suggests that thousands of young people who do not fit the narrow categories accepted as being owed the main homelessness duty go unrecorded as a result, even if they have been rough sleeping. They report that more than 150,000 young people ask for help with homelessness every year (Centrepoint, 2016).

Homeless Link (2015: 3) research indicates a difference in the scale of youth homelessness reported by homelessness providers and that reported by local authorities, with 68% of providers reporting an increase on 2014. In August 2015 a provider survey indicated that nearly half of those living in homeless accommodation services were aged between 16 and 24 (Homeless Link, 2015). However, over the same period, local authorities reported a reduction from 31% to 20%. A possible explanation for this difference is

> that fewer young people are approaching their local authority for support and are approaching providers, or that young people are being signposted to providers as part of their local authority's advice or prevention.
>
> (Homeless Link, 2015: 3)

Again, accurate assessment of the numbers involved is clouded by categorizations and the ways in which homeless young people may fall between two or more areas of support or intervention. However, the scale of youth homelessness is indicated in key findings from research carried out by Clarke *et al.* (2015):

- around 83,000 homeless young people have been accommodated by local authorities or homelessness services during 2013–14
- there are around 35,000 young people in homeless accommodation at any one time across the UK
- 26 per cent of UK young people have slept in an unsafe place because they had nowhere else to go. This equates to an estimated 1.3 million young people aged 16 to 24
- 20 per cent of UK young people have experience of sofa surfing, which would suggest over a million 16–25 year olds having done so nationally.

A link between multiple forms of disadvantage and homelessness has been identified and discussed above. Research for the Joseph Rowntree Foundation found that the mix of people in poverty has changed: there has been a shift towards younger, working people in private rented accommodation (MacInnes *et al.*, 2015). Other research (Wilson, 2016: 1), building from the Department for Communities and Local Government data, showed that

> [t]he ending of an assured shorthold tenancy (AST) has been the most frequently occurring reason for loss of a settled home in the last 17 consecutive quarters. 32% of all homeless acceptances in England between April and June 2016 arose from the termination of an AST, while in London the figure was 41%.

The welfare reforms announced in the 2015 Summer Budget and the Autumn Statement of the same year have had particularly marked consequences for out-of-work single people aged 18–21 who, subject to specific exemptions, may be entirely excluded from support with their housing costs or otherwise subject to the very low shared accommodation rate of housing benefit in the social as well as the private rented sectors.

Clapham *et al.* (2014) considered the housing pathways of young people in the UK housing market and their situation as either 'in the social queue' or 'chaotic'. Young people in the social queue pathway, which comprises 1 million young people, have been raised in the social rented sector. The research found that interviewees generally aspired to have their own tenancies in the rented sector. The research also highlights the risk that members of this pathway will find great difficulty in gaining adequate housing and may end up experiencing homelessness and thereby moving into the chaotic pathway. The chaotic pathway is marked by repeated entry into and exit from the social and private rented sectors. For this vulnerable group, Clapham *et al.* (2014) also found initial exit from the parental home is often into homelessness and is most frequently caused by family conflict. Homeless Link (2015) confirm this finding and have found that being unable to remain living with parents or care-givers is the single biggest cause of youth homelessness. It has already been shown that local authority support and intervention are limited for this particular group, with no one set of data being able to confirm the exact number of homeless young people. Numbers can reflect those who are known to the services but cannot determine the full scale of homelessness. According to a recent estimate based on a bespoke telephone survey, as many as one in five young people 'sofa-surfed' during 2013–14 (Clarke *et al.*, 2015), a figure that can give only an indication of the scale of the issue.

Homelessness also tends to be a gendered experience. The largest group to be consistently eligible for assistance, unintentionally homeless and in priority need are lone females with dependent children. This group made up 47% of the total number of homeless people in this category between July and September 2016, representing 7,090 people (DCLG, 2016a: Table 781).

Official government statistics highlight regional variation in homelessness (ibid.); Nottingham City is one local authority with high levels of homelessness.

Homelessness in Nottingham

The population of Nottingham stands at approximately 319,000. Of this number 22% (just over 71,000) are aged between 16 and 24. Government data shows that Nottingham is one of the 20 local authority districts with the highest proportion of neighbourhoods in the most deprived 10 per cent of neighbourhoods in England on the Index of Multiple Deprivation (IMD) 2015 (DCLG, 2015a).

Individual, interpersonal and structural factors play a role in the causes of homelessness. Nottingham has several structural features that can influence young people's outcomes as represented in the IMD score. Fitzpatrick (2005) summarized a 'new orthodoxy' that has developed in theorizing homelessness that attempts to combine 'structure' and 'agency' by demonstrating how structural disadvantages restrict an individual's capacity to respond to personal problems and tragedies.

Bramley *et al.* (2015) have provided a statistical profile of a key manifestation of severe and multiple disadvantage (SMD) in England. Nottingham City Council had the eighth-highest prevalence of SMD based on three national data sources for England in 2010–11 (see Table 2.1).

Table 2.1 Prevalence of severe and multiple disadvantage in Nottingham, 2010/11, by three data sources and combined

Data source	Supporting People Programme	Offender Assessment System	National Drug Treatment Monitoring System	Combined
'Prevalence rate' per 1,000 working-age population	260	199	181	213

Note: The national average is 100.

Source: Bramley *et al.* (2015: 22).

In conjunction with the IMD score, the SMD score calculated by Bramley *et al.* (2015) provides an overarching picture of deprivation within Nottingham City. While it is acknowledged that high levels of deprivation exist in pockets across the city, other measures of deprivation (e.g. low academic attainment) also point to an area that requires significant levels of intervention. It is perhaps not surprising that the number of people accepted as being homeless and in priority need for the financial year 2015–16 is 4.61 per 1,000 households. In the previous year, the number accepted as homeless was 4.1 per 1,000 households (DCLG, 2016a: Table 784).

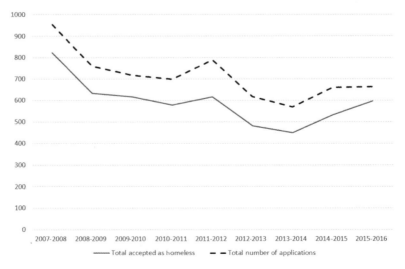

Source: https://www.gov.uk/government/statistical-data-sets/live-tables-on-homelessness

Figure 2.1 Homelessness applications and decisions

In order to access support provided by the local authority, people need to apply to have their homeless status recognized. Figure 2.1 (on previous page) shows the numbers of applications and 'accepted' decisions, that is, recognized homeless, between 2007 and 2014 in Nottingham. Of the accepted applications, families with dependent children are the most prevalent group accorded priority need in Nottingham. In the 2013–14 period, 318 households (representing 71% of the total acceptances) submitted successful applications.

This pattern is consistently repeated. During the period July to September 2016, a total number of 92 families with dependent children (representing 88% of the total acceptances) formed the largest group accessing local authority services. Of this number, 66 were headed by lone female parents, again mirroring the national picture for this group. The greatest number of applicants fall into the 25–44 age bracket. However, 23 young people aged 16–24 (representing 21%) were considered eligible, unintentionally homeless and in priority need at the point their application was accepted from July to September 2016. This number is not insignificant in the context of Nottingham's SMD and IMD scores detailed above.

Homelessness and young people in Nottingham

The level of child poverty in Nottingham is worse than the England average: 35.2% of children aged under 16 years live in poverty. The rate of family homelessness is also worse than the England average (Public Health England, 2014). Despite this data, the picture did appear to improve slightly in 2015. During snapshots of homelessness presentations across the City and County of Nottingham, Nottinghamshire Homeless Watch recorded a total of 509 households as homeless during the two-week period in which the questionnaire was implemented. The results of this survey showed a decrease over the previous two years and the lowest figure recorded by this survey. Throughout the time that the survey has been carried out, the most recent increase in support needs has been in the area of mental health, as illustrated in Figure 2.2.

Of the 509 people seen in the 2015 survey, nearly one-third were sleeping rough, over a quarter were under 25 (16–24: 45 male, 62 female). The main reason for homelessness was cited as 'parents no longer willing to accommodate', which has remained consistent in every year the survey has been completed.

Nottingham City recorded 228 homeless presentations. The 82 women seen in the city accounted for 51% of all female presentations across both Nottingham City and the county, the highest proportion recorded by the survey. Seventy-one rough sleepers were seen, representing 45% of the total rough sleeper count (Nottingham Homeless Watch, 2015).

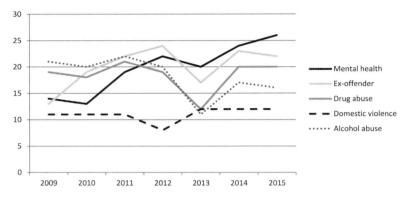

Source: Nottinghamshire Homeless Watch (2015).

Figure 2.2 Main five support needs 2009–15 by percentage of presentations

Nottingham City Council (2015) asserts that it has a commitment in accordance with the Southwark ruling that any 16- or 17-year-old presenting as homeless will be given a package of support regardless of the outcome of their Child in Need assessment. The 2009 'Southwark Judgement' stated that homeless 16- and 17-year-olds should now be treated as 'children in need', with a full social services assessment that includes their care needs. The City Council states that in an emergency it is likely that accommodation will be arranged by Housing Aid, including use of hostels, emergency rooms and Nottingham Nightstop. Nottingham Nightstop provides emergency overnight accommodation, in the homes of trained volunteer host families, to young people aged 16–25 who are on the point of becoming homeless, on a night-at-a-time basis. It received 327 referrals for young homeless people during 2011. Nottingham Nightstop reports offering 1,146 nights of accommodation between 2006 and 2011 to vulnerable homeless young people (Nottingham Workplace Chaplaincy, 2012). Longer-term accommodation arrangements include placements with relatives and supported accommodation via the homelessness prevention gateway, where homeless individuals can remain until they are aged 18.

The homeless are also supported through the work of Framework, a charity and housing association that operates in the region. Framework have reported that 31% of their service users in 2014 were aged 16–24, 1% being aged 16–17. A higher number of service users was reported by Nacro

Young Person's Accommodation, with 49% of the service users being aged 16–17 (Nottingham City Council, 2014).

Conclusion

Homelessness is a complex issue compounded by various forms of disadvantage. It is evident from official data that homelessness frequently follows family disruption, including at times violence. While the majority of homeless people tend to be aged 25–44, the second-largest group to record as homeless is aged 16–24. Despite some improvements in the numbers reported as homeless during the Labour Government, subsequent governments have failed to address this issue with similar levels of urgency. Further, specific policies have resulted in an increase in the numbers of homeless people requiring support. Nottingham City has high levels of deprivation as identified by a range of outcome measures, including academic attainment, employment levels and housing. There are numerous pockets of disadvantage within which high levels of crime are reported, including drug abuse, theft and other more violent types of crime. It is in this context that a consistent number of young people find themselves homeless and in need of local authority intervention each year. In addition, poor mental health has consistently been cited as an area of support need for young people accessing local authority support.

Chapter 3

Exploring Homelessness: Who cares?

Introduction

Homelessness in the UK remains an embarrassing inconvenience. Outside of academia and charitable work it is rarely spoken of and there seems to be a prevailing reluctance in government and wider society to acknowledge it even exists. When homelessness *is* recognized it is often presented as a problem of personal incompetence rather than as the product of deeper structural issues of inequality which might have created or at least contributed to the situation. On a personal level, families too often struggle to openly accept the role they may have played in constructing circumstances which have caused homelessness. This institutional and domestic lack of acknowledgement, together with individual personal hesitance to report homelessness, means it is difficult to define the scale of the problem accurately. Consequently, homelessness remains a largely hidden societal dilemma.

This chapter looks beyond simple explanations of youth homelessness and considers who should take responsibility for helping young people to gain permanent settled accommodation. The chapter examines the roles of government and the voluntary sector, and also the assumed responsibilities of families. It reviews the different housing options open to young people, and explores The Positive Pathway, an innovative government/voluntary sector initiative designed to tackle youth homelessness.

Youth homelessness: who really cares?

Rather than being considered a vital resource needed for the future economic well-being of a nation, young people are often presented as a drain on society, responsible for the rise in criminality and the decline of general standards. If young people become homeless, their situation is presented as one they have personally caused through their own ineptness. This is a convenient, simple explanation which does not explore the complexity of the situation; nor does it recognize the many stages that may have led to a young person's losing their home. It is important to recognize that '[b]y the time a young person becomes homeless, they are likely to have already been through several crises in their lives. These may have included school exclusion, running away, involvement with social services or the youth justice team, or the introduction of a new step-parent' (Cullen, 2004: 12). In the same way that homelessness reflects a multi-stage breakdown of support at the individual and organizational levels, there are also opportunities, at any stage prior to the loss of accommodation, for positive intervention which could help to prevent homelessness.

The process of caring for young people and supporting them to make a successful transition into adulthood is shared between different individuals and organizations. A young person's initial carers are assumed to be his or her birth family. In the absence of a caring birth family, the government, via its various agencies, assumes this role, and at different points various voluntary sector organizations, driven by a philanthropic agenda and supported by the government, may become involved. Each of these groups has a positive role to play in supporting young people towards independence. If a young person leaves their home in an unplanned manner they face the real risk of becoming homeless. Consequently, dedicated, innovative solutions are needed to stop youth homelessness becoming a depressing inevitability. The challenge for the future is how birth families, the government and voluntary sector organizations can work together to prevent youth homelessness.

The role of the family

Families are configured as the primary building blocks of society and are required to provide safe, secure and stable care for children and young people. In the UK young people are expected to remain in the family home until they are old enough and sufficiently competent to accept responsibility and care for themselves. Young people are supposed to leave home in a planned manner, supported by their families and given the opportunity to return for guidance and possibly financial assistance as and when needed. Their families are also expected either to help young people to find appropriate, safe accommodation or to guide them to agencies that can help in this endeavour.

The role of the government

Historically, systematic state support for homeless youth and destitute children was clarified in the 1601 Poor Relief Act. Under this legislation, parish councils could collect local taxes to support the poor of the parish. In the later seventeenth and early eighteenth centuries many councils decided the most effective way to provide this support was in a single institution, commonly known as the workhouse. In these establishments young people were fed, clothed and given an elementary education; when they were old enough they were trained for a trade so they might find gainful employment. However, conditions in workhouses were harsh: children were separated from their parents and allowed only limited contact with each other; residents were made to work for their board, and punishments were draconian. Consequently, workhouses became feared institutions which poor people sought to avoid. Nevertheless, the workhouse system continued in some parts of the UK until 1948.

Even in contemporary times not all young people are fortunate enough to be cared for by a loving family. Through a combination of circumstances some become the responsibility of the state. Some are forced to leave their family home because it is no longer safe, others have no relatives who can look after them. In these circumstances the government becomes the young person's 'corporate parent' and via the local authority assumes responsibility for their care. Under the 1989 Children Act (revised 2008), the local authority must allocate a named social worker who will determine the young person's needs and suggest plans for their immediate care. This may involve being fostered, living in a local authority children's home or, if it is safe, returning home. Even though local authorities are empowered to make interim arrangements, all long-term or permanent care proposals must be agreed and ratified by the courts. These include adoption and special guardianship arrangements.

The role of the voluntary sector

Voluntary organizations, including charities, have a long history of being involved in youth care in the UK. The first dedicated children's home, the Foundling Hospital, was established in 1741 by Thomas Coram for the care of deserted and orphaned children. Over time other philanthropists became involved in looking after abandoned children and provided funds either to open orphanages or to support homeless youth. These include such well-known figures as Dr Barnardo, who opened his first home in 1870 and adopted the motto 'no destitute child ever refused admission'. Barnardo's closed its last residential care home in 1989 and now focuses on intervention and support work, such as vocational training, parenting support and abuse prevention.

In the past care for homeless young people has been shared between government and the voluntary sector. However, as the 'number of local authority children's homes has shrunk' (Berridge *et al.*, 2012: 5) the role of the voluntary sector in providing accommodation for homeless young people is likely to become more important. In addition to accommodation, modern voluntary sector organizations offer many other services to support young people, including mediation, counselling, budgeting advice and help finding employment. Furthermore, there is 'evidence that a voluntary sector input' (Whalen, 2012: 15) is particularly effective in helping to combat youth homelessness.

Can homelessness be prevented? The Positive Pathway Initiative

The Positive Pathway Initiative is a fusion between the government and the voluntary sector that provides a creative solution to youth homelessness. The Pathway gives a coherent response to youth homelessness and a framework for tackling this problem. Working in partnership, St Basils (a Midlands charity) and Homeless Link (a national charity with links to local and national government) developed a Positive Pathway model to try and prevent youth homelessness. This eight-step model provides a structure to work with young people and their families over an extended period of time. The model adopts a multi-agency approach and seeks to engage different partners, who can work with young people to try and stop them becoming homeless. Positive Pathway aims to:

• prevent a young person from initially losing their home, through education and crisis reduction
• offer an integrated service gateway where young people can access support and guidance on potential housing options
• provide access to different types of fixed-term supported accommodation
• propose longer-term settled accommodation.

Positive Pathway places young people at the centre of all decisions while striving to enable young people to take control of their lives. This model was so successful in the West Midlands that it informed the government report 'Making Every Contact Count' (DCLG, 2012a: 15), and the Conservative/Liberal Democrat Coalition Government (2010–15) committed itself to 'fund the St Basils youth homelessness charity to promote use of the youth accommodation pathway and innovative approaches to youth homelessness, working with local authorities and leading voluntary sector providers over 2012–13' (ibid.: 16) on a national basis. It is expected that all local authorities will adopt this framework to help them combat youth homelessness.

While the eight steps of the model remain constant, the types of support accessed at each step will vary depending on how the young person became homeless, their last accommodation, their existing support networks and their needs. The eight-step Positive Pathway framework (illustrated in

Figure 3.1) has been used to examine young people's changing support needs and to demonstrate which individuals and agencies can care for young people at each step. Not all young people will need to utilize all eight steps, and some will be able to successfully establish settled accommodation at an earlier stage in the pathway. Although development work is still needed at some steps of the pathway, the model retains its significance because it provides a coherent structure for tackling youth homelessness and provides options for working with young people in complex situations.

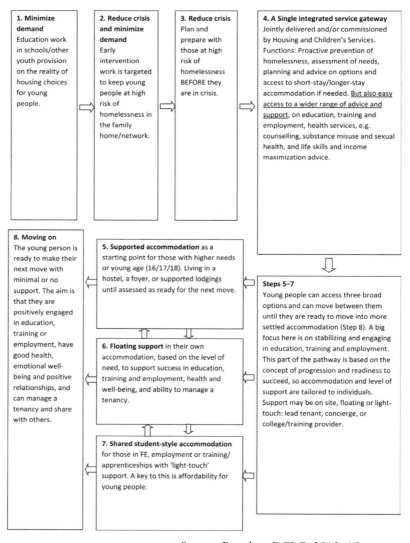

Source: Based on DCLG, 2012: 15.

Figure 3.1 The Positive Pathway Model

Step one: minimize demand

The first step in helping a young person to avoid homelessness is to ensure they are fully informed of the realities of living independently. It is reasonable that as they mature young people will develop their own ideas and test family boundaries, and might behave in ways that are difficult to manage. It is also possible that the constraints imposed by families will seem intolerable to young people, who may make different choices. However, while there may be internal family disagreements, they need not result in homelessness.

Some young people mistakenly believe that if they leave their family home they are automatically entitled to housing from the local authority. While local authorities have an obligation towards a number of different vulnerable groups, including young people, families and pregnant women, if the young person could safely have stayed in their family home and there was no irretrievable breakdown in relationships, the local authority does not have to accommodate them. This belief may result in young people placing themselves in potentially dangerous situations, such as sleeping rough. If a young person leaves their home when they could have remained, social services will most likely return them to their family home even if the young person does not wish this to happen. Young people need to be informed about the risks, dangers and responsibilities of leaving home, and families need to be guided on how they might resolve their differences so that young people can remain in the family network.

Compulsory education has a key role to play in the reduction of housing demand and the prevention of homelessness before it starts, by working with younger people and informing them of their housing options. However, it is important to remember that not all schools follow the national curriculum or deliver Personal, Social and Health Education (PSHE) sessions. Although most schools can see the place for teaching about the hazards of substance misuse, in an increasingly crowded curriculum some schools may view housing sessions as dispensable. Further education (FE) colleges (which work with students as young as 14) are also not required to follow a statutory PSHE programme, and while youth work teams could help to explain to young people what it means to leave home, attendance at a youth group is optional.

Although the Positive Pathway has been adopted by the government as a model of good practice, at this stage it has no legislative authority. As a result, schools, colleges and youth support services are not obliged to provide young people with information on the risks and dangers of leaving home. Equally, there is no co-ordinated mechanism to advise families on housing options for young people and no central guidance on domestic conflict resolution which could help to reduce homelessness.

Step two: reduce demand and crisis

Some young people are at high risk of becoming homeless. Many of these young people and their families are already known to local authorities. This group includes care leavers ('30% of homeless people have been in the care system'; Who Cares? Trust, n.d.), people who have had difficult education careers or 'poor attendance at school' (Homeless Link, 2014b: 13), people who have been involved in crime ('Of the total number of young people who approached local authorities or providers for help with homelessness during August 2014, 13% were young offenders'; Homeless Link, 2015: 11) and substance abusers. Consequently, young people may already be working with a variety of agencies, including Children's Services, Youth Offending Teams and other support organizations.

Work at this step of the pathway focuses on early identification of the young people at greatest risk of homelessness. At this point the aim is to implement appropriate intervention strategies with pre-17-year-olds, either to help them remain safely at home or to support them in a planned exit. This stage requires co-ordination across a variety of services so that there is continuity and young people benefit from consistent advice. Intervention strategies at this stage might include, for example, mediation services or parenting advice. However, in some local authorities there has been a lack of coherence across services, or suitable help has not been provided in a timely manner. This breakdown in cross-service support can contribute to youth homelessness.

To provide support for the highest-risk groups and to promote inter-agency collaboration, the government has implemented the Troubled Families programme (DCLG, 2012b). However, this programme is based on a 'something-for something' approach, and full funding is only provided in arrears once agreed outcomes for young people have been achieved. Furthermore, the programme is only intended for 120,000 of the most challenging families and ignores many other young people. While this programme may be useful for some, it may not offer appropriate support to young people not from troubled families.

Step three: reduce crisis

Although it is desirable that young people should remain at home wherever possible, in some circumstances this is not achievable. There may have been an irretrievable breakdown in communication or there could be issues of safety. It may be impossible to accommodate a young person within the extended family network; in such a situation the only feasible solution is for the young person to leave. If this is the case, it is better to plan their exit than to leave the situation until a predictable crisis occurs which culminates in homelessness and acrimony.

Even in hostile environments many young people appreciate the opportunity to maintain controlled family contact. A planned exit provides the best opportunity to preserve what may be fragile relationships and to allow the young person to gain greater control over their situation. While it is likely that a young person will need some form of additional support, a planned exit gives support agencies an opportunity to put appropriate assistance in place. Again, some form of mediation may help the young person build positive family relationships, or active engagement with youth work teams help them establish support networks outside the family base.

Step four: single integrated service pathway

One of the principal challenges that young people face is finding out what support is available and where they can access help. It is easy for young people to feel lost in the range of professional services or become confused by the array of advice they may receive. Often, young people who become homeless need support in a number of areas if they are to be successfully rehoused and keep their accommodation.

An integrated service pathway would help to remove or minimize some of these difficulties by presenting a single contact point for young people to access different services and to gain help from different providers. The key agencies at this stage in the pathway would be 'Children's Services and Housing working together' (Whalen, 2012: 15). These two agencies would co-ordinate the support needed and signpost additional services from other providers, which might include education (for example life skills courses at local FE colleges), information about welfare rights (for example benefits advice from organizations such as the Citizens Advice), emergency accommodation when there is a risk that a young person has nowhere safe to stay and health (including guidance from groups such as AddAction, a national specialist drug and alcohol treatment charity).

Steps five to seven: accommodation options

Depending on their individual circumstances and level of need, young people will need access to different accommodation options. The steps at this stage of the pathway are not hierarchical and young people should access the option most suited to their needs. They may also move between the steps and may need temporarily to be given more support if they experience a crisis. Different accommodation options are effectively the final staging post before a move into settled accommodation. Ultimately, the final goal for all young people is the same: progression into stable, enduring accommodation where they have full control of their housing.

Step five: supported accommodation

Supported accommodation should be provided to the most vulnerable young people and those with the highest level of need. This is the most costly of all accommodation options because of the level of input needed from a variety of professional services and is in limited supply. Young people could be living in foyer accommodation (see Chapter 10) or supported lodgings, or possibly with another family. At this step young people need help in a variety of ways, which might include budgeting, managing their tenancy and daily living. They are helped to develop the skills they need to move on to a more self-sufficient lifestyle. Support is available throughout the day over the whole week, either in person or via a telephone help line. Only a small number of the most needy of young people can expect to remain in this sort of accommodation for a long period of time (more than two years); most will, after assessment, progress to more independent housing.

Step six: floating support

Floating support is suitable for young people who have low to medium levels of need. They will be in their own accommodation and will have some, but not necessarily all, of the skills needed to live independently. Variable support will be tailored to individual need, depending on the young person's progress and their readiness to move into fully independent housing. Support moves beyond a focus on housing alone, and young people are encouraged to explore education, employment and personal welfare issues. There is no fixed time for this sort of support, although the intention remains to prepare young people for independent living as soon as practicably possible.

Step seven: shared student-style accommodation

This type of accommodation is suitable for young people with a low level of need who can largely operate independently and only need help in specific areas. Support at this step could be provided by floating support or some other provider such as the local college. Alternatively, this type of accommodation may be suited to those who have spent some time in fully supported accommodation and are now able to cope with less intensive assistance.

Sharing with others has many benefits for young people as they develop their independent living skills, including learning how to work in groups, extending their own personal support networks and reducing isolation. Unfortunately, this type of housing is in short supply and many private landlords are reluctant to rent to groups of young people. Some local authorities have recognized this gap and are working with the private sector and social housing to develop options for shared accommodation for young people.

Step eight: moving on

This step represents the ultimate goal for all young people: they will be in secure, settled accommodation provided by either social housing or the private sector, managing on their own. While this remains the ambition for all young people, some will struggle to make the transition and will continue to require help as adults.

Conclusion

> Young homeless people are arguably one of the most vulnerable groups in society and continue to make up a significant proportion of clients who access and receive support from homelessness services in England ... Without adequate support, homelessness can significantly affect young people's lives. Young homeless people are more likely to become homeless again when they are older, and also face greater difficulties finding work.
>
> (Homeless Link, 2015: 6)

Youth homelessness continues to be a national problem. Figures for January to March 2012 indicated that 'statutory youth homelessness has ... increased significantly, by 8% .... 4390 households headed by a 16–24 year old were accepted as statutory homeless' (Brown, 2012), while in 2013–14 an estimated '83,000 young people were in touch with homelessness services' and during the same year there was a '40 per cent increase in the number of 18–25 year olds sleeping rough in London since 2011/12' (Crisis, 2016b: 56). Without structured, positive intervention, numbers of these young people will struggle to 'secure both work and reasonable, affordable ... accommodation' (Quilgars and Pleace, 1999: 110). Without employment and accommodation, it is difficult to establish a base and to be an accepted member of society; in effect, an excluded underclass is created.

The eight-step positive pathway model is not a panacea which will end youth homelessness, but it is a coherent multi-agency framework that provides a structured approach to tackling this dilemma. It draws together resources from family and friends and voluntary-sector and government organizations, and provides a co-ordinated approach that uses the strengths of different agencies. Although this model has great potential it lacks legislative authority, and while the Conservative/Liberal Democrat Coalition Government (2010–15) committed to supporting St Basils and Homeless Link to deliver a national roll-out of this model, no statutory timescale was drawn up detailing when local authorities would have to have structures in place. In a cash-poor, economically driven environment where local government is constantly trying to make savings, it is easy to envisage a situation where the needs of homeless young people will not be prioritized and their needs will continue to be neglected.

Chapter 4

Listening carefully: Finding ways to support young people telling their stories

Introduction

This chapter will describe how the research was undertaken, from its inception to its current status. It details the ways in which the two researchers entered the field to ensure the boundaries normally associated with research could be minimized. The chapter includes a description of preliminary fieldwork, which included establishing a climate conducive to discussion. We trace how we came to understand the context within which we aimed to gather data. For example, we quickly discovered that no topic was considered out of bounds from the young people's perspectives. We also found that we needed to revise our understandings of the young people and to learn their language so that we and they could communicate with each other effectively.

The process involved in deconstructing the information gathered will also be covered, through discussion of our reflections in the car before and after the interviews. We will talk about the ways in which we tried to engage the young people through humour and through recognition and acceptance of difference. Given the complex nature of the issues faced by this group of young people, we also discuss the challenges associated with not overtly displaying shock when participants described their use of drugs and alcohol, their sexual habits and their history of abusive relationships.

To support the young people as they told their stories we deliberately utilized silence to provide an opportunity for the interviewees to collect their thoughts so that they could accurately express what they wanted to say. When they seemed to be struggling to capture the right word, we offered alternatives, checking with them whether they were the best words to describe their experiences. In attempting to further support the story-telling process, we offered examples of our own problematic experiences, hoping that some common ground could be established as we teased out painful memories of particular episodes in their lives.

Nottingham Community Housing Association

As Chapter 2 states, homelessness is a particular issue for young people living in Nottingham: a significant number of young people experience homelessness in the forms identified in that chapter. Nottingham has a range of supportive mechanisms which young people can access; the Nottingham Community Housing Association is one such site.

The Nottingham Community Housing Association (NCHA) was founded in 1973 and is now one of the largest locally based housing groups in the East Midlands, managing over 8,100 homes and housing more than 15,000 tenants in Nottinghamshire, Derbyshire, Lincolnshire, Leicestershire, Northamptonshire and Rutland. Its reach extends across the East Midlands and it supports 2,095 young people. The work of the NCHA covers mental health, learning disabilities, domestic violence, Asian elders, vulnerable young people, homelessness, teenage parents, older persons, provision of housing and support in clients' own homes.

The sample

A sample of convenience was established through direct communication with the NCHA's key workers across the various sites.

The sample comprised 15 young people, representing half the residents in one housing association and a quarter of those in a second. The gender mix was: 5 females; 10 males. The participants were aged between 16 and 19. The study was made up of two phases. The participants in Phase 1 were young people who were accessing NCHA services. The participants in Phase 2 included peer mentors (young people currently living in NCHA accommodation or who had previously been tenants) and three NCHA staff.

As with any research with marginalized groups, it often happened that when we arrived at the housing association the individual we had arranged to see did not attend their interview slot. Although we had numerous 'wasted' visits, we appreciated that our interview would be low on their list of priorities. It therefore made perfect sense that some of the scheduled interviews did not take place. We had to remain patient and reschedule, knowing that flexibility in our approach to the young people would be of importance. We made clear to all participants who we were and what our role was, and that we would not be able to provide solutions to their difficult life situations but could provide a space within which they could voice their experiences.

Identifying with the sample

Before we conducted the research, we both had some connection with the sample through their own social histories. One of us had experienced a short period of homelessness as a result of a problematic relationship with her sole parent. The period of homelessness was extremely brief, in part because of the ways in which the benefits system worked at the time, and also because of social connections who passed on appropriate knowledge about how to access the required support. The experience of coming from a dysfunctional broken family had left its mark and was a point of connection with the sample. However, it would be disingenuous to make claims of connectedness with the sample in the study. There is now much distance between the former and present self and the 'dialectic between connection and otherness that is at the center of all forms of historical and cultural representation' (Behar, 1996: 20) served as a reminder of the complexity of researching the experiences of those whose present experiences reflected a lived past.

The other, as a member of a Black minority group, has experiences of being marginalized and battling racial stereotypes and prejudices. We were therefore not coming at this research from a naïve assumption of objectivity – we recognized that we would hear elements of individual narratives that could provoke memories of painful experience from our own pasts. Behar (1996: 13) states, 'it does require a keen understanding of what aspects of the self are the most important filters through which one perceives the world and, more particularly, the topic being studied.'

For us, this was important. We needed to understand how our past experiences could influence the research, and the filters that would inevitably colour the ways in which we questioned, followed up areas of interest and responded to the narratives of the participants as they unfolded. We were also acutely aware of the need to remain as objective as we could in order to achieve the appropriate balance between 'connection and otherness' (Behar, 1996: 20). As individuals who had 'struggled with great social challenges in the past but [had] now overcome them' (Deuchar, 2009: xi), we appreciated each other's roles in drawing out the narratives of the young people in the study.

Preliminary scoping

> [N]o person undertaking research with highly marginalised young people can fail to be aware of the importance of building strong relationships with research participants.
>
> (Couch *et al.*, 2014: 19)

We were both mindful of the potential difficulties we faced in securing the young people's trust and the importance of building a relationship with the participants. We had been informed by the Housing Association that the young people in their care were reluctant to talk, even to their care workers. It became apparent that we needed to undertake preliminary visits to familiarize ourselves with the context that we were entering and to each become a 'familiar' face to the occupants. This work took place over three weeks: we visited the research sites and sat in the communal spaces. We did not use these visits as formal data collection activities, but more to become part of the furniture, albeit in a limited way. During our visits, young people would enter the communal area: some would ask who we were and what we were doing, but generally we were ignored.

Establishing a presence within the context was important: we were appreciative of the target group for the research and sensitive to their lack of trust in people they did not know. We used the preliminary visits to chat informally to whoever wished to chat with us and provided cakes as a way to break down any potential barriers. We had been informed by the housing association staff that cake would be an effective way of encouraging the young people to chat with us. We were not aware of how effective this activity had been until we later entered the field to undertake the formal interviews.

Our preliminary visits provided us with some general insights into the lives of the young people, which we reflected upon when travelling to and from the research sites. These conversations became useful in helping us consider the extent to which we were able to tease out the narratives of the young people and also provided a space where we could begin to make sense of what was being said.

The young people appeared to have no boundaries in what they spoke about. Drugs, alcoholism, violence became key themes of informal discussion. In this context, we were cognizant of issues in relation to potential disclosures that would need to be reported. While care workers were always in the immediate vicinity when we were chatting with the young people, we were particularly troubled by some of the stories we were exposed to. We were mindful of Behar's (1996: 2) concern with the role that researchers play in the field:

> [A]s a storyteller opens her heart to a story listener, recounting hurts that cut deep and raw into the gullies of the self, do you, the observer, stay behind the lens of the camera, switch on the tape

recorder, keep pen in hand? Are there limits – of respect, piety, pathos – that should not be crossed, even to leave a record?

It was important for the research project that we maintained an objective stance and did not display shock when we were told of, for example, abuse and extreme violence. However, that did not mean that we were not affected by what we were being told during the course of the interviews: our car journeys became increasingly important, as a way in which to obtain some distance from what had been said but also for agreeing the boundaries that we would impose on the research and our responsibilities to the young people.

We visited three sites, as we wanted to ascertain whether there was any difference between young people's narratives in city and rural locations, particularly in relation to their educational experiences, but also in relation to how the housing association was supporting them.

Operating ethically

> The nature of ethical problems in qualitative research studies is subtle and different compared to problems in quantitative research. For example, potential ethical conflicts exist in regard to how a researcher gains access to a community group and in the effects the researcher may have on participants.
>
> (Orb *et al.*, 2000: 93)

Working with vulnerable groups brings particular challenges. Of primary importance to us was that our presence should not exacerbate the young people's situations. Hugman *et al.* draw our attention to the importance of operating ethically in research with marginalized groups:

> Ethics in social work research increasingly recognises that the rights and interests of subjects must be primary. The principal aim is to ensure that the subjects of research are protected from harm that might result from their participation in the research.
>
> (Hugman *et al.*, 2011: 1271)

Knowing that the young people in this study had a background of instability in their family backgrounds, which led to their needing the services of the NCHA, we were aware of the need to go beyond the institutional processes usually associated with working ethically. Thomson (2016) highlights the danger that institutional ethical approval processes will only offer a superficial nod towards ethics: 'permission-oriented paperwork doesn't go near all that is involved in an ethical research practice'. There was, of course, the need to comply with institutional ethical approval processes, which are closely aligned to the guidelines produced by BERA (2011). But, as experienced researchers, we both knew that we would be dealing with a vulnerable group and could address areas of their lives that had caused, and possibly continued to cause, them upset. Pittaway *et al.* (2010: 231) remind us that 'the ethical challenge is for researchers to add value to the lives of the people they are researching, recognizing them as subjects in the process and not simply as sources of data.'

While we were mindful of this, there was no escaping the parameters of the research endeavour: we knew we would be collecting their stories and that these would constitute our data. However, the emphasis we placed on facilitating a space through which the young people felt empowered to recount their histories, albeit partial histories, was such that we went beyond viewing the participants simply as sources of data. We briefly discuss the aspects of our own backgrounds that provided a point of connection with the participants later in this chapter, but, more than this, we entered the research field with

> a framework for being able to make use of the common connections of human values, such as honesty, respect, privacy and so on, so that [we were] able to negotiate processes and outcomes that both protect[ed] and promote[d] the interests of participants and ensure[d] that methodological rigour [was] maintained.
>
> (Pittaway *et al.*, 2010: 242)

We appreciated the importance of gaining the young people's trust and of implementing strategies that could reduce our 'outsider' status. While gaining access to the sites for the research was unproblematic, gaining access to the 'research community', that is, the young people themselves, was more challenging. As Couch *et al.* (2014: 18) point out, 'The most difficult aspect of [the research] and the first stage in the research process lay in the "outsider" gaining entry into the research community.'

We knew that some of the individuals participating in the study would be engaged with, or would have been engaged with, activities that could be criminal, such as drug taking or selling, grievous bodily harm, actual bodily harm or theft. As we went through informed consent with the young people, we explained the confidential and anonymous nature of the interview. The participants have been given pseudonyms. We also made it clear that we would have to report, as appropriate, any information (about criminal activity, for example) that could result in them being at risk.

In order to create the most appropriate context in which we could interview the participants, we visited the various settings over a period of three weeks and undertook some preliminary scoping. This had the dual effect of enabling us to become more familiar to the potential participants and allowing us to gain some sense of the field that we would be exploring.

Adopting a qualitative approach

We were interested in finding the most effective way of facilitating discussion. While we had a series of questions we wanted to put to the young people, we quickly established an approach to the interview that enabled us to follow up points of interest with them.

The most important aspect was to establish trust from the beginning. We did this through humour and being informal with each other: talking over each other, finding ways of laughing at ourselves and each other, and so on. This appeared to work and the young people appeared to respond to us positively.

The qualitative principles we applied to this study placed an emphasis on:

> phenomenology, with importance placed on the experiences and voices of individuals, and a belief in multiple realities; the value of research as a participatory process; the importance of researchers' reflexivity; and the inevitability of researchers' subjectivity and, hence, the need to make that subjectivity overt during all stages of a project.
>
> (Couch *et al.*, 2014: 16)

Hearing the stories from the point of view of the participants and in their own words was particularly important for us. We therefore adopted a semi-structured interview approach. In line with the body of research related to student voice (see for example Cook-Sather, 2006; Fielding, 2004), we wanted to remain true to the participants and reflect their stories in the ways that they wanted to recount them. As a consequence, we have quoted the participants' words verbatim.

In addition to the semi-structured interviews conducted across both phases of the research, the following data was collected as part of Phase 2:

- existing numeric data on numbers of peer mentors
- existing numeric data on numbers of mentees

- survey data from mentors
- entry and exit surveys from mentees.

Phases of the research

The research had two main phases:

- Phase 1 placed a focus on exploring the educational experiences and aspirations of the young people.
- Phase 2 explored the homeless young people's experiences of an internally developed peer-mentoring programme.

Data collection took place over a period of seven months.

Questions for the participants (Phase 1)

Questions that framed the interviews were constructed and agreed with staff at Nottingham Community Housing Association. The NCHA was keen to explore whether they were having any impact on re-engaging the young people with education. As a result, the main research question for Phase 1 of the study was:

> What is the impact of NCHA support on the educational aspirations of young people?

While the NCHA agreed the questions (see Box 4.1) that underpinned the interviews, we were struck by the way in which the conversations with the young people in the study veered away from the set questions. Responses in some cases were very brief, even monosyllabic. Despite further prompting and probing, some of the young people were clearly not in a place where they could open up fully. In such circumstances, we posed other questions in an attempt to help the young person to open up. This was not always entirely successful; some participants continued to provide mono-syllabic responses.

> **Box 4.1 Phase 1 questions**
>
> What educational achievements do you already have?
>
> Have you ever been diagnosed with/Do you think that you have a special educational need such as dyslexia, ADHD, learning disability?
>
> What was school like?
>
> If you stopped going to school/college, why?

Do you hope to enter back into/continue with education? Why?

What do you want to do later in life? What are the barriers to this?

Do you work or do you want to?

Do you live in/come from a city/town/village?

What is the educational background of your family?

What is the educational attainment and aspiration of your peers?

What do you think about your friends who are on courses/in work?

When did you decide that this was your path (e.g. school isn't for me, I'm too thick for college, I'm going to get a degree, I'm going to do a vocational qualification, etc.)? Were there any key people who influenced this decision (e.g. parent, teacher)?

What impact does having your own licence/tenancy have on your educational aspiration?

Is education a priority for you?

Do you use drugs or drink alcohol? When did you start? What impact has this had on your educational aspiration/attainment?

Questions for the participants (Phase 2)

Phase 2 of the study focused on the internally developed peer mentoring programme. The questions that framed this part of the data collection are shown in Box 4.2.

Box 4.2 Phase 2 questions

How successful is the peer mentoring programme in supporting vulnerable and disengaged young people?

In what ways has the programme facilitated change for vulnerable and disengaged young people?

What change is evidenced six months after involvement in the peer mentoring programme?

What change is evidenced one year after involvement in the peer mentoring programme?

The questions for participants during Phase 2 of the research project were also agreed with NCHA staff. They are shown in Box 4.3.

BOX 4.3 PHASE 2 PARTICIPANT QUESTIONS

What made you want to become involved with the Wavelength peer mentoring project?

How often have you contacted your dedicated mentor?

How often should mentoring take place?

How long should the sessions be?

Whose responsibility is it to set up sessions?

What do you feel about attending the mentoring sessions?

What difference have the mentoring sessions made to you?

How have the mentoring sessions helped/hindered you?

What sorts of topics have you covered in the sessions?

Do you feel you could have made the same progress without the sessions?

What are your current/future plans?

Have your plans/aspirations changed as a result of mentoring?

How would you feel if mentoring stopped now? What difference would this make to you?

How will you know when you are ready to stop being mentored?

Was your mentor the same race/age/gender/sort of person you are? Does this matter?

What would your ideal mentor be like?

Have you stopped doing anything because of mentoring?

Have you started doing anything because of mentoring?

Has mentoring changed the way you think of/see yourself?

Have your friendship groups changed because of mentoring?

Has your accommodation changed because of mentoring?

Can you name three really good things about mentoring?

Can you name two things that would be improved about mentoring?

If you had to appear on East Midlands Today to talk about Wavelength mentoring, what would you say?

Limitations of the study

The limitations of the study come from both the sample and the sometimes closed nature of the participants' responses. It was evident that these young people were extremely guarded in what they said and a small number would not go into detail about their experiences. During the process of the research, it became increasingly apparent that their experiences had been so traumatic that they had become 'closed': they would only reveal the level of information they wanted to in relation to the personal aspects of their lives (e.g. home, family), whereas other elements, such as drug taking, did not evoke the same level of guardedness. The extent to which the participants revealed their run-ins with the police or dangerous situations they had found themselves in had no boundaries. We understood this as being an area of perceived success and identity formation. The young people had lives built on chaos and disorder, and inhabited this fact through their narratives. We were not able to ascertain the extent to which they might have been exaggerating their experiences in the hope of impressing us, or indeed how accurate their reflections were. Given the insights we were provided with, we agreed early on in the research process that we would take the young people's stories at face value and not question the 'truth' contained within them. We adopted the view that, even if the stories had been exaggerated, the way in which they were told represented the truth for the young person.

Understanding the stories

The narratives were transcribed and subjected to thematic analysis. The following themes emerged from the data:

- experiences of education
- family breakdown
- misplaced family loyalties
- personal resilience
- aspirations for the future
- the role of housing projects
- the role of peer mentoring.

These themes form the basis of the following seven chapters. In exploring the themes, we illuminate the intersectionality between them and how these factors ultimately led to homelessness and the young people's current situation.

Conclusion

Carrying out research with marginalized groups presents many challenges. Some of those challenges have been noted above. Building rapport with the young people was critically important to the success of the interview and we attempted this through preliminary scoping visits. In addition, once the interviews commenced we used humour and being open to any questions the participants posed to us as vehicles through which trust could be established quickly. While preliminary visits added to the length of the research project, as Couch *et al.* (2014) found, they were extremely valuable to the collection of data, and also to our understanding of the data. Some participants provided very brief responses to questions. Again, this is a feature of working with vulnerable young people. While we did prompt and ask for more information, we also had to intuitively understand when such prompting needed to stop to ensure no harm came to the participants. We were keen to represent the young people as they presented their stories. This meant remaining true to the language they used, and so quotes presented in the following chapters are not filtered in any way.

Chapter 5

'I got kicked out of every school': Young people's narratives of their educational experiences

Introduction

This chapter focuses on the young people's educational journeys before they became homeless. It indicates the mixed bag of experiences that framed the young people's relationships with education from primary through to post-compulsory education and other educational provision. It portrays the interrupted and broken educational careers of young people as they moved between schools and, at times, around the country. It depicts the ways in which they negotiated their paths or were directed through the differing sectors. The young people's accounts of their educational experiences mainly illustrate progressive alienation, although this was not the case across the whole sample. At the point of their need for NCHA intervention, all of the young people in this study were not engaged with education.

Disadvantaged young people and education

It is well documented that young people who experience multiple forms of disadvantage invariably struggle with school (see for example Wedge and Prosser, 1973; Billington and Pomerantz, 2004; Barnes *et al.*, 2006; Platt, 2011). The young people in this study are no exception to this. Central to their problematic relationships with education were feelings of alienation, unaddressed specific learning needs, challenging relationships with teachers and limited ideas about the purpose of education for their future lives. The young people in this study described feeling disconnected from school at an early age, viewing it as a burden in their already complicated lives. However, they also recognized that their future lives were somewhat dependent on being successful in education. This tension revealed itself in many ways, but mainly through persistent limited engagement, disruptive behaviour, truancy and low attainment. Their stories about their educational experiences reflect a resigned helplessness in the face of processes that pitched them at the margins of schooling. Their attempts to fit into school were frequently thwarted by the reality of their home lives, which led to a cycle of expulsion and disrupted education.

Despite struggling with a system that seemed to have formulated preconceived ideas of homeless young people's abilities, some young people managed to retain or rediscover a route through education which was consistent and appropriate to their personal educational needs. Some of the young people turned to significant others who helped them understand the potential value of education in assisting them to achieve life goals. However, this was not reflected across all of the narratives and was more the exception than the rule.

Feelings of alienation

Education is viewed as a conduit for social mobility (DfES, 2003; DfE, 2016), but the link between various forms of disadvantage and poor educational experiences is well documented (see for example Bourdieu and Passeron, 1977; Reay *et al.*, 2005; Burgess and Briggs, 2006). The inextricable link between poverty and educational failure is identified as a particular issue and highlighted in government data that evidences year-on-year low achievement in areas of disadvantage (GOV.UK, 2016). Being successful in education is not just a matter of ability but is linked to wider sociological debates, including perceptions of fit and belonging but, more than this, the idea of what constitutes normality and conformity. As Aaltonen (2012) states,

> The strong emphasis placed on educational achievements as a precondition for successful adult life in Western societies attests to the fact that school plays a significant role in setting the standards for normality and conformity among young people today.
>
> (Aaltonen, 2012: 219)

Young people who do not conform to expected standards of behaviour become constructed as 'other', and their lack of fit results in them being 'classified as problematic from the school's point of view' (Aaltonen, 2012: 219). The young people in this study recognized a sense of alienation early on in their educational lives. Roy explained that he was part of a group that was largely ignored by the teaching staff in his school:

> They spoke to us alright, do you know the low-grade ones, they wasn't bothered about us too much, they were just like doing

all the high grades, they concentrated on them a lot, a lot more than us lot.

This sense of not mattering in school was a consistent theme within the young people's narratives. The process of alienation (Bourdieu and Passeron, 1977) was evident across the data set, although how this occurred differed. Natasha, for example, became difficult for her teachers at secondary school. She stated:

> I was alright in primary school and everything and then I went to high school and I was alright for the first six months of Year 6 and then I just started being a little trouble maker ... always getting kicked out of my lessons ... misbehaving and being gobby ... just arguing with my teachers, thinking I'm right and they're wrong. I've never really got on with teachers.

This feeling was echoed by Bella, who also described a problematic relationship with teachers:

> I used to get in a little bit of trouble ... I don't know really. I was just skiving lessons and stuff because I didn't really get on with the teachers.

Getting on with teachers was critical to whether the young people felt able to engage with their educational setting. Chad explained that he generally got on with teachers:

> I was okay with teachers, the mardy ones, the nice ones, but I still used to get along with them all.

Despite the positive relationship Chad appeared to have with his teachers, he described a problematic relationship with school and constructed his sense of identity in relation to what he knew he was not. He developed the idea that he was not able to fit into mainstream school and was deserving of a place in a facility that catered for naughty boys: his behaviour in this context made him stand out as different from that which is expected and controlled in mainstream schooling. His sense of identity was being framed by the peer group that established the cohort for the 'special school' he was sent to. In this context, Chad identified as one of the 'naughty boys', a label that also emphasized his inability to cope in mainstream education:

> Where I was, it was like there was no naughty girls, so it was just naughty boys that used to go there. Like if you couldn't cope in mainstream school, you used to go there.

His further alienation from school was evident in both his behaviour and his approach to attendance. Chad has a history of non-attendance and regularly truanted from school. He did not value its role in his life and did not have any aspirations that could give any meaning to attendance.

While in the 'special school', Chad recounted further difficulties with one of the boys that contributed to his ongoing feelings of isolation and disaffection with education:

> It's like I was there and I kept bumping in to this one guy every day and we disliked each other and we used to fight. I nearly got arrested because of him, it was lucky that the head teacher stopped us. I was going to kill him. I had a metal blade in my hand. Not very good. I'm not a nasty person, like, it's just I can only take so much.

Chad's experiences of school left him feeling 'on the edge' much of the time. He was unable to find a mechanism through which he could establish a fit either socially or educationally and the structures within his particular education system seemed to reinforce his feelings of isolation. There is a sense that comes through in his narrative that the school's attempts to correct his behaviour did quite the opposite. Chad was not able to explain why this was the case, and he was not the only participant who engaged in destructive behaviours.

Destructive behaviours

A consistent pattern of destructive behaviour was seen across the sample. The young people in this study faced considerable challenges in their personal lives, including difficulties with their home backgrounds. It is perhaps not surprising that comments relating to social background would provoke a reaction. This was the case with Tony, who was unable to control his emotional responses to consistent references to his family:

> It's stuff that they say to you obviously. I was in care when I was younger and people say stuff about my family and stuff and I don't like that. I was in care, I didn't see them. I had ADHD and so I just trigger easier and then I just flip out.

Tony struggled with his identification as 'the kid in care' and was unable to cope with the constant reminder that there were perceived issues with his background. He would 'flip out' because he was not able to respond in any other way. Deuchar (2009: 6) informs us that the most pronounced risk of falling into teenage delinquency and youth violence arises when young people live in low-income, stressed and isolated families or where poverty and unemployment are combined with lack of parental social support.

This would certainly appear to be the case for Tony, whose troubled past included a range of factors indicative of a disadvantaged background. Tony has lived in care since the age of six and 'got moved around a lot'. His response to frequent periods of change and instability, along with his identified ADHD, caused him to display challenging behaviour and violence:

I had ADHD as a kid and I was in a court school, it's called the court school, it's like for kids that have behaviour problems and stuff … I got chucked out of every school I was in when I was younger, so I wasn't very good in school … I would just fight everyone [including teachers].

Over time, Tony learnt to limit the impact of his behaviour and avoid confrontation by removing himself from a potentially difficult situation:

I didn't truant, it was just if a teacher shouted at me I would just walk out of the class. I would just go to time out because that is where they would usually send me.

This strategy appeared to work in the short term. It provided him with a sense of control as he had self-determined when to leave a lesson, but it also helped him to avoid escalation into violence. He did not like being shouted at by teachers, but this was a frequent occurrence as his behaviour continued to decline. What is perhaps surprising is Tony's refusal to truant. Despite the constant challenges he faced at school, it was the only place that offered him some sense of stability. It is evident from Tony's narrative that he struggled with not seeing his family and with the sense of isolation he felt as a result:

It's just stuff – because I was living in [place name] and so I didn't see my family for years, so it was just getting to me, that's all … I just didn't know them. Like I haven't got a secure place. That's what I've been trying to get since I was younger, but, it's just the system is not very good.

Arnold *et al.* (2009:7) state:

Segregation, exclusion or removal from the environment in which children behaved differently was still at the heart of intervention. The range of possible separations can still be found in modern systems.

Tony's recourse to violent behaviour led to him eventually being excluded from school. Chardonnay also displayed behaviours that challenged teachers and resulted in her exclusion:

> I got kicked out of everything there [High School]. I wasn't allowed in mainstream school … I was just a brat. [I whacked] some trampy girl. I pushed [a teacher] out of the way … I got told I did. I couldn't remember. The teacher told me I did. [When I get angry] I just can't remember what happens.

Chardonnay reflected on her younger self in a way that acknowledges a difference from what she had become. She likened her behaviour to that of a 'brat', although she further explained that her outbursts had been in response to another pupil, who had called her names. A pattern of segregation, exclusion and removal from the environment emerged from what the young people said as the main method for dealing with their problematic behaviours. Such removal contributed to the ways in which the young people understood themselves and constructed their identities. Chardonnay explained:

> I was in the annexe. That's when you can't go to mainstream school. It's like another school, you do all your lessons in there and that's it. I preferred it … it was just easier. They just give you a book and you just learn out of the book.

Reintegration into mainstream school was gradual and dependent on good behaviour: pupils would 'get their lessons back' as they began to display more acceptable behaviours. It was particularly evident that the experience of being isolated from the 'normal' pupils contributed to the ways in which the young people viewed themselves and their abilities. There was a sense in which the period of time away from mainstream education had left its mark on the young people's identities. They were unable to construct an identity of belonging and, their difficulties compounded by their complex life situations, struggled to find a sense of fit. The rigidity of the system could only deal with the challenges presented by the young people in one way: to remove them from mainstream education. However, as Aviles de Bradley (2011: 155) points out,

As the numbers of homeless children and youth continue to rise, it is imperative for educators and others to understand the experiences of unaccompanied homeless youth.

It is important to note that while the majority of the young people in this study experienced challenging educational journeys that resulted in academic failure, this was not the case for all of them. The next section details two young people within the sample who appeared to go against the grain and buck the trend.

Bucking the trend

The link between multiple forms of disadvantage and education failure is well documented and referred to above. It therefore came as no surprise to us that the majority of young people in this study experienced academic failure throughout their schooling experiences. However, what did take us by surprise were the experiences of Sarah and Clark.

Clark recounted an education history that did not appear to align with his current situation. He was sent to an independent high-achieving high school where he successfully completed 10 GCSEs, achieving '3 A*s, 5 As [and] 2 Bs'. Following this set of results, Clark moved on to a sixth-form college, where he struggled.

> I just struggled ... once I left school – because [name of sixth-form college] was like a bigger environment and I got diagnosed with dyspraxia. It's hard to like organize and put things into place so when I went to college obviously A levels are more, you've got to do more of your own work if you get what I mean? Whereas school is like structured, this is what you've got to do. That's probably what I'm more suited to, do you get what I mean? When I've got specific targets, whereas A levels I struggled a bit and I was like missing school and things like that so I didn't end up completing my A levels.

Despite this setback, Clark continued to make decisions in relation to his future. This forward-looking perspective was something that did not feature in discussions with other young people in the study. From what he said, it is apparent that Clark had the ability to evaluate his position and he had very clear ideas of what he wanted to do, and, perhaps importantly, what he felt he was suited to. Clark detailed how he took control of his situation and recounted how he secured a place in an FA coaching programme:

Emmm, well football has always been something I've wanted to do and I've sat down and thought I would prefer to work in an environment which is more, you know, like going out into schools or something and doing coaching rather than being in an office, or working in a call centre or something like that because of my concentration. I would prefer to be doing something more active really. So last year I looked for like funding opportunities on the internet and found this charity – it's called the Lawrence Atwell's Charity and they like fund educational courses for young people around the country. They're based in London. So I applied to them, they gave me the money, I went down to Hertfordshire; they paid for like all the hotel and all that kind of thing …

There are many aspects of Clark's narrative that indicate his self-reliance and ability to search for opportunities. When asked how he knew about such schemes he responded with:

I know these things. I know how to research for funding and grants and stuff. Like at the moment, or next Thursday, I've got an interview in London and it's called the Winston Churchill Fellowship. I've been shortlisted for that, I beat about 1,000 people and that's to do a project to go to Brazil to work in the favelas, you know with gangsters and stuff like that, because what they do is they take this like gang members and teach them how to coach football, so then they become role models for the young people and it kind of ends the cycle if you get what I mean.

Clark's experiences provided us with an 'outlier' which we could not easily explain. His history and his capacity to plan for his future contradict much that has been written about young people who find themselves in similar situations. While the distance Clark feels from his family is evident in the absence of any reference to them as he discusses his future plans, it is perhaps the inheritance of various forms of capital through his family history that has enabled him to take control of his situation. As Bourdieu (1990: 54) states,

The *habitus*, a product of history, produces individual and collective practices …. It ensures the active presence of past experiences, which … tend to guarantee the 'correctness' of practices and their constancy over time ….

When Clark does include any reference to his family, it is in relation to perceptions held of his ability to manage during difficult times:

> I think at the moment it's like a new focus. Like if I haven't got a focus or something to work towards I can just become like – in fact my dad always says I just bury my head in the sand. I just go into myself and I'm not engaging with people or I don't want to speak to people and go out. When I've got a focus that's it. I know where I want to go and that's it and no one can really stop me but it's just about keeping that mindset really.

Clark's narrative recognizes the need for focus and is indicative of a self-reliance that is unusual within this group. Instead of being identified as a helpless victim, Clark has developed, or possessed, the attributes required to enable him to make decisions, take control of his situation and improve it.

Sarah's story is one of partial difference from the norm of this group. Her family background is typically associated with the middle class (based on socio-economic classifications (SEC)). However, her current estrangement from her family had positioned her in less favourable circumstances, where her future was less secure. She, like Clark, achieved much success at GCSE, achieving A*–C grades in eight subjects. When recounting her academic credentials, Sarah indicated that she was 'supposedly' good at maths. When this was probed further, she explained:

> I was also doing an A level a year early in mathematics. Yeah, supposedly [I'm good at maths]. Well the problem was, the reason supposedly is because I was supposed to get an A and then I got a C overall, so supposedly, so I'm retaking that this year to get an A.

Built on an ambition to go to the University of Cambridge, Sarah's commitment to study and her determination to be successful influenced her approach to revision:

> Yeah but like I'll lock myself in my room and do revision for eight hours solid, I'm that sort of person. I plan to complete my A levels – I hope to get enough grades to go to Cambridge Uni.

Family background also appeared to influence Sarah's capacity to consider her future. Her father is a paediatric psychologist and her mother completed a degree; both influenced Sarah's positive attitude towards education. Despite Sarah's aspiration to go to Cambridge, her journey towards this goal has been interrupted by her current situation:

> Kicked out of my parents', I'm still at college, but it's kind of
> on special circumstances because of what's happened. But I was
> doing Further Maths, Maths, English Lit and Law, and I dropped
> Law quite quickly because I realized I didn't like how they were
> doing it really, at all, and then I carried on Further Maths and
> English but then after being kicked out for quite a few months,
> I just dropped so far behind on those subjects, because of like
> stress and stuff. I'm only doing Maths again this year.

When asked whether she felt she would be able to secure a place at Cambridge, Sarah had 'no idea', but was relying on her 'special circumstances' as a way of securing a place.

The impact of being homeless and requiring the intervention of the NCHA indirectly helped the young people back into education. For Clark and Sarah, intervention took a different format from the usual. It was primarily focused on supporting them in their search for information to support their ideas about what their next steps would be. This theme is picked up in more detail in Chapter 9. For the majority of the young people in this study, the intervention of the NCHA enabled them to navigate their way onto courses at local colleges, with varying levels of success, both in accessing courses and in their completion.

Education and second chances

Whether the young people responded positively to the prospect of returning to education depended to a large degree on how they had been able to deal with their troubled histories. Tony, for example, had a particularly troubled past which had led to him being violent. He was able to consider a return to education and a possible future because:

> I don't know, I've grown up. It's like the experience you have in
> life. It like proves who you are as a person when you get older.
> Everyone has got problems, it's just that you get over some of
> them don't you.

However, as Tony continued to talk about possible engagement with education, it became clear that he had experienced issues with the 'second chance opportunities'. This was in part because he had been required to study English and maths, which he didn't enjoy, but also because of organizational problems:

> I've done sports courses before. I can't finish them. I don't know
> what it is. Every time I've done something they've either put me

in late or it's something else. I did a training course with [name of local organization] but it was a 10-week course and they put me in like five weeks in and they expected me to catch up with them, with the amount of work that they were doing anyway.

The limited engagement Tony demonstrated with his second chance was influenced by how he understood himself and his educational history. He did not actively seek out his key worker's support in securing an educational experience, as

I'm really not bothered … I don't have a plan because that's meant to be in your head from school, isn't it? … But I've never done job experience or anything like that so I haven't had a plan since never. I didn't have that experience. I didn't have that chance.

Tony established himself as 'other' in relation to how he perceived futures get played out. In his view, it is 'normal' to have a plan from an early age and also to build that plan from 'job experience'. Given the disruption to his education and the lack of job experience, Tony feels that any second chances within education are pointless – he simply has too much to catch up on and feels overwhelmed.

In the same vein, Chardonnay left school with no qualifications and worked closely with her key worker, who had tried to facilitate a return to education in the preceding September. Chardonnay had a young child of ten months and had felt that 'he was too young to be left'. It became clear that her child provided a sense of purpose and was a priority even when other important things needed to be completed. For example, she was planning a return to education to study for an NVQ later that year. When asked about the course, Chardonnay was unable to detail its content or the level at which she would be studying. She had been unable to attend the information event and explains:

I was meant to go on Tuesday morning at nine a.m. but I couldn't make it because he was poorly and full of [a] cold.

She hoped that this course would eventually lead to her securing a university place to complete a nursing degree. It was clear that Chardonnay relied on her key worker to advise her and that the key worker was 'helping me get back in college in September'.

Key workers provided a vital 'gateway' to impenetrable information. They frequently contacted college tutors on behalf of the young people. At times this required them to act as advocates of a young person at risk of being excluded. An important aspect of their role appeared to be to break the cycle of isolation and exclusion from education, although this proved challenging at times. Natasha's key worker was influential in securing her a place at a local college to complete a hairdressing course. This 'second chance' was proving successful, as Natasha felt more at home in that environment and enjoyed the way in which material is taught. As she explains:

> I think it's because I'm doing something that I actually want to do so I won't get bored of it, but I think whereas at my other schools and that, because I didn't have no interest in it whatsoever, I used to act up and play up and everything. But if I do something that I like and it's practical, instead of sitting there writing loads of letters and everything out, then I'm sort of alright with it, as long as I enjoy it, I don't really get a problem.

There was a sense in which the young people were realigning themselves with a system that they had experienced as a form of alienation. Previous encounters with education had resulted in their 'elimination' (Bourdieu and Passeron, 1977: 153) in one form or another. The 'second chancers' were not only trying to secure academic qualifications, but also attempting to repair the damaging messages about themselves they had acquired as a result of their previous negative experiences.

Conclusion

Despite struggling with a system that at times seemed to evidence preconceived ideas about homeless young people's abilities, some participants managed to retain or rediscover a route through education which was consistent with and appropriate to their personal educational needs, and aspirations if they held them. Young people recounted stories of significant others who helped them to understand the potential value of education for helping them to achieve other life goals. While the young people were well supported by their respective key workers, it was evident from their narratives that they continued to experience education as a site of tension.

Chapter 6

'I just told my Mum, if this carries on, you're going to lose a son': Family breakdown

Introduction

'Most young people who are homeless leave home because of a breakdown of family relationships' (Arthur, 2007: 23), and the young people in this study all recounted problematic relationships with family members. Central to their eventual homelessness was a myriad of differing points of family breakdown including single catastrophic events, and the more invidious cumulative attrition of trust and security. These events combined to cause pivotal moments of family relationships breakdown. The young people became detached and unlocated, unable to make sense of their own place in their families. Their stories reflect a continuum of dysfunctionality where the young people endlessly searched for ways to resolve their difficult home situations but were unable to do so.

Many young people exhibited a real crisis of identity as they experienced the principal carers in their lives abandoning them. This often began with a disconnection in childhood, developed into adolescent alienation and matured into full-blown hostility as they grew older. The scars of this life journey were evident as the young people depicted their childhood experiences, and yet they still craved what they perceived to be a close 'Disney' family ideal. This chapter explores the role and concepts of the family as a unit, the accepted principles of family life and the ingrained assumptions about the roles within families.

The chapter considers the challenges and choices faced by young people and the rationality of leaving the assumed security of family life for the uncertainty of homelessness.

Family life

While the ideal of the family is a familiar concept, how families are constructed and how they function is different in and unique to each unit. The idea of the nuclear family, comprising a mother as the care-giver and homemaker, a father as the protector and provider of material necessities and children as helpless creatures to be moulded in the shape of their parents, is one that has maintained popularity since Victorian times. In contemporary times 'this specific model of family life has achieved wide currency' (Wright and Jagger, 1999: 19) and has been reaffirmed by 'the tabloid press and traditional Conservative politicians' (Peart, 2013: 124), who assert that this is the *only* acceptable model of family and parenting. Families that are constructed in this way are valued by society because they have 'good parents ... who have happy, healthy, safe and successful children' (Warner, 2006: 65), children who will later become useful members of society and model citizens. By default, families that are constructed in any other way must have bad parents who produce bad children who go on to become the scourge of society.

While most young people in this study desperately sought the popularized assumed normality of a nuclear family, their personal lived experiences did not conform to this idea. Further, census data indicates the nuclear family 'is rapidly becoming a historic concept which does not fully reflect the way families are constituted in the UK today' (Peart, 2013: 124). The last full census in 2011 recognized six different types of family groupings, namely married couple family, married couple stepfamily, cohabiting couple family, cohabiting couple stepfamily, lone mother family, and lone father family. Although couple families (whether married or co-habiting), which represented the sought-after norm, still formed the largest group of all family types, from 2001 to 2011 the percentage of couple families as a component of family groupings hardly rose at all. By comparison, the percentage of lone-parent families (either lone mother or lone father) rose significantly. In 2001 there were 2,363,306 lone parent families, 16% of all families. By 2011 this figure had risen to 2,892,293 families, 18% of all families (Office of National Statistics, 2014), the majority of which were headed by mothers. Few of the young people who took part in this study reported leaving homes with happily married parents who preserved traditional roles and functions. The 'normal' experience of family life for these young people was living either with a sole parent, in a dysfunctional couple family, or in care.

While the 'rise in cohabitation, divorce and lone motherhood are ... lamented because they are seen to represent a decline in adherence to a particular *ideal* of family life which involved marriage as a lifelong commitment' (Featherstone, 2004: 19), because of archaic attitudes families which deviate from the classic, nuclear family 'are held as problematic and undesirable' (Wright *et al.*, 2010: 60) or 'dysfunctional' (Mirza, 2009: 55). Even though lone parenthood is now the fastest growing of all family types, families that are constructed in a non-traditional way are configured as a threat, capable of undermining and disrupting the 'very fabric of society' (Jagger and Wright, 1999: i).

Families, regardless of construction, are considered the primary building blocks of society. Consequently, families and family units are charged with a number of significant responsibilities designed to preserve social stability and security, and promote future economic prosperity. In order to achieve these goals families are expected to:

- Give structure and order to domestic life and provide a base from which children may become enculturated into prevailing societal norms. In this respect the family represents a microcosm of wider society in which roles and responsibilities are allocated, rules are enforced and consequences for non-adherence to regulations are enacted.

- Ensure children have a permanent safe location from which they can develop. While, over time, there has been an extension of 'state involvement in welfare' (Bochel, 2008: 192), for example in education and health, the state does not expect (or want) to take primary, daily responsibility for child rearing. This task is, except in unusual circumstances (for example wartime or the death of all known genetic relatives), routinely allocated to the family unit, and the state supports the position that it is in the 'best interests of most young people aged 16 or 17 to live in the family home' (DCSF, 2010: 3). When traditional family units break down, the state prefers to house young people aged 16 or 17 'with responsible adults in their wider family and friends network' (ibid.). When this is not possible the state does all it can to create newly formed family units through fostering, adoption or special guardianship arrangements.

- Provide children with 'appropriate moral values' (Wright and Jagger, 1999: 19), including transmitting 'fundamental British values' (DfE, 2014: 5) through fitting adult role models so that children can understand accepted standards of behaviour and develop 'positive and healthy identities' (Wright *et al.*, 2010: 60).

- Produce 'socially competent children [able] to navigate social worlds effectively and develop independence' (Warner, 2005: 76). While families are responsible for providing a base, their primary goal is to create self-sufficient adults who are not reliant on state support.

- Prepare children to enter society and make a meaningful social and financial contribution.

The nature of lone parenthood, and potentially being removed from extended families, means that single parents have less access to support systems and other resources which could help with childcare responsibilities. Lone parents frequently have less financial resources and are 'nearly twice as likely to be in poverty as those in couple parent families' (Gingerbread, 2017). However, in terms of childcare and child rearing duties, societal expectations are identical for single parent and couple families. These expectations place a considerable burden on lone parents which sometimes results in complete family breakdown.

Causes of family breakdown

Families provide the security children need to develop into responsible adults. In part, this security is achieved through feeling 'loved and appreciated, and [being] a valued part of a family group which is ... related to a wider social network' (Harris, 2011: 35). Unfortunately, not all young people are assured of this stability; the young people in this inquiry witnessed their families being dismantled or disintegrating through a catalogue of internal incidents or outside interventions. When families broke down, the young people in this research lost hope and an understanding of their place in the world. They no longer knew where they could find support and whom they could trust. They became rootless and suspicious of authority and authority figures who had failed to provide them with the structure and stability they needed.

The impact on children and young people of family breakdown can be profound, creating feelings of 'sadness, grief, anger and resentment [and] many feel an increased vulnerability and uncertainty' (Allan, 1985: 113). This was powerfully expressed by Tony, who recounted how his family had been broken up:

> I was in care and I got moved around a lot from about 6. I was living in different places and I didn't see my family for years. I was put into a care home. It was getting to me. I didn't know them. I haven't got a secure place. That's what I've been trying to get since I was younger. My brothers and sisters are all in care and we've all got separated. Four of them are living with my mother but I don't speak to my Mum. My two older sisters were put in care as well but they got adopted.

Although Tony was not able to provide details on why he and some of his siblings were placed into care, since 1989 (at which time Tony would not even have been born), under the provisions of the Children Act, local authorities have only removed children from their parents' care when there has been a risk of significant harm and all other avenues of family support have been exhausted. For Tony and his other siblings to be placed into care suggests that his family were, at that time, unable to offer an adequate, nurturing home environment. Because Tony was removed from his parents' care in childhood, he never had the opportunity to form early 'healthy relationships with authority' (Harris, 2011: 101), develop a sense of self, or have the security needed to explore the world from a safe, caring base. As Tony grew older and matured, his feelings of distrust grew so that he presented as a young man who seemed to have given up on life and appeared to have nothing worth striving for. Tony's problems were magnified as a result of his frequent moves, which continued to trouble him as he tried to navigate his route into adulthood.

While it may be difficult to define a '"right age" for young people to leave home, ... there is increased [government] concern to prevent young people from "leaving home prematurely"' (Jones, 1995: [2]). Although Tony presents as an extreme case, having been taken into care as a child, other young people who leave home prematurely increase their level of personal risk as they enter uncertain environments which may not provide the security they need or crave.

However, some young people have no choice and 'are forced out of their homes' (Nebbitt *et al.*, 2007: 546) as a result of escalating internal conflict, violence towards them or other family members and changes such as divorce, separation or the introduction of a new adult partner. In these circumstances young people can either endure a hostile, toxic environment or make a rational choice to leave the family home.

Some of the more common causes 'that triggered their actual transitions into homelessness' (McNaughton, 2008: 55) are now discussed.

Family conflict

Family hostility and intense arguments 'between young people and their parents or guardians' (Greve, 1997: xiv), were the most common cause of leaving home. The nature of arguments varied, but all showed a trend to becoming more intense over time until they became intolerable. For many of the young people in this study hostility had become a mundane part of daily life and they expected conflict at home. This situation is vividly illustrated by Tom, who was living in a couple stepfamily when he first left home.

> On my 16th birthday I had an argument with my mum and my stepdad. She pushed me through the front door and I fell

backward through the glass. Mum rang the police and said I did the damage and I was in a cell for the day. My mum and me, we never had a bond. My dad came and got me and I moved in with my dad. My dad and stepmum were arguing all the time. My stepmum was 'Either he goes or I go', and I said 'Well I'll just go' and I moved in with my sister.

Tom felt he never developed an 'attuned relationship' (Harris, 2011: 101) with his mother and did not seem to have that sense of attachment usually seen towards mothers. This pattern of parental distance continued throughout his life and he did not develop close, stable bonds with either his birth parents or his step-parents. Arguments in Tom's family resulted in him living with four different family units, his original dysfunctional birth family, a first stepfamily, a second stepfamily and then a sibling, as he sought a permanent base. However, each family unit was less secure than the previous one and finally Tom, having failed to find the haven he needed, left to live independently. Tom expressed his constant disappointment with parental and sibling support as follows:

My dad let me down loads of times. So has my mum. That's how it was with me pretty much my whole life with my dad and my mum. My sister had really bad depression and I was looking after her more than she was looking after me. When you're with someone like that all the time it starts bringing you down.

Even though it meant an uncertain future, living independently became the only viable housing option for Tom and as a consequence he made the logical decision to leave home.

Violence

Violence was another common cause of family breakdown; 'experiencing abuse is a frequent explanation for homelessness' (Arthur, 2007: 23). The young people in this study were able to recount tales of being attacked and attacking others. As is often the case in domestic violence offences, these events were not usually reported to the police and families elected to keep these incidents silent, perhaps in the hope of a later reconciliation or because the young people themselves recognized the 'potential impact of disclosure on themselves, their family and abusers' (Franks *et al.*, 2015: 152). However, while keeping silent may have been motivated by a wish to protect themselves or family members, it also prevented opportunities for professional intervention to help build positive family relationships. Ranjit, Roy and Chardonnay shared three very different stories of family violence.

Ranjit, a young Asian male, described a particularly difficult home environment where his mother was the perpetrator of sustained physical and emotional abuse. Research has shown that, possibly as a result of the pressure of trying to raise a family alone, 'single parents were more likely to hit and abuse their children' (Gelles, 1997: 59). Although Ranjit did not claim to be the victim of sexual abuse, his words did not exclude this possibility. Ranjit's circumstances seemed especially complex as he could not understand why he was singled out among his siblings for direct attack. The violence seemed to isolate Ranjit and he internalized his situation, accepting responsibility for causing the aggression by stating that he had always 'been the odd one out'. His isolation was further exacerbated as he had no one he could easily talk to about his experiences for fear of 'adverse consequences for family honour' (Mullender *et al.*, 2002: 134), and other Asian families 'had already had negative experiences of breaching confidentiality' (ibid.). This reluctance to disclose or confront aggression served to 'compound the oppression of domestic violence itself' (ibid.: 135) and to allow attacks to continue. Ranjit's situation was even more complicated as wider society tolerates and even colludes with 'parental rights ... while imposing strong sanctions against children' (Gelles, 1997: 109). Eventually Ranjit ran away to escape his brutal home background. When he returned, at his mother's request, she seemed to punish him for challenging her authority by running away, and resumed the attacks. Ironically, Ranjit's mother's final punishment of throwing her son out finally enabled him to find safe accommodation.

> My family was violent with me. I was abused in both ways and obviously I ran away from home, but my mum wanted me back, so I went back and it started happening again and then I just told my mum, 'If this carries on you're going to lose a son'. So after that she started getting really violent and she kicked me out. I didn't have anything wrong with me, but I still got kicked out.
>
> (Ranjit)

Roy, like Ranjit, had left home because of violence, but it was Roy who had been responsible for attacking his father. Roy accepted responsibility for his actions and was aware he had created problems in the family home.

> I got violent with my dad over drug issues. Weed. I literally got crazy with him and ended up smacking him. After, I just got

> kicked out. Dad didn't want me at the house when I done that, so
> I went into hostel living.
>
> (Roy)

After leaving home Roy had been able to maintain contact with his family and while it 'took a little bit of time to get back talking' with his father, relations had improved. Because 'children abusing their parents is so counter-normative it is extremely difficult for parents to admit they are being victimised by one of their children' (Gelles, 1997: 109), and this may have contributed to the family's unwillingness to report Roy's violent behaviour. However, Roy gave the impression that throughout his difficulties, in an open display of support, his whole family continued to be concerned about his welfare. Roy had kept in regular contact with his 'nan, uncle and all that lot' and had a confidence that he could turn to his family, including his father, who remained a significant figure in his life, whenever he needed to.

> I got a carer, my dad, you know caring for me. If I need to, because
> my dad knows loads of stuff, I'll go and ask him.
>
> (Roy)

This reliable base gave Roy the assurance he needed to plan for his future, and he was learning to cope and looking forward to new possibilities, including employment.

Chardonnay described an unusual experience of family violence, in which her formerly aggressive father became less violent so that he might have access to his two daughters.

> When my dad was younger he used to be violent and stuff until
> he got me and my sister and that was when he calmed down.

Once he had secured custody, Chardonnay lived in the family home with her father and sister but lost all contact with her mother.

In each of these stories, direct violence was the catalyst for family breakdown. Families were fractured and children either left or were thrown out of their family home. In only one of these three narratives, Chardonnay's, was it possible to rebuild the family unit and reunite children with their parents. This demonstrates the lasting impact of family violence.

Changes to family organization

Chad described how his parents split up while he was still an infant. Chad knew there was a custody dispute between his mother and father, and after court intervention his father was granted full custody. This is noteworthy.

While the purpose of the family courts in the UK is to ensure the ongoing welfare of the child, custody is more frequently awarded to the mother. Further, the family courts would always seek to preserve relationships with both parents through contact arrangements, recognizing that secure, caring relationships are vital for child development. The lack of contact arrangements with Chad's mother suggests there were significant issues with her ability to provide adequate care for her son. Since his parents' separation, Chad had lost contact with his birth mother. He explains:

> Mum and dad separated about 15 years ago. My dad went to court saying he wants full custody of me to spite my mum. I don't know what happened from there, I just remember growing up with my dad.

Over time, however, relationships between Chad and his father broke down and eventually he became homeless.

Mental health issues

Mental health issues were a further cause of family breakdown. While the young people seemed aware of the mental health concerns of other family members, they did not seem ready to acknowledge that they also might have mental health problems or that the stress of their later homelessness might create personal 'emotional and behavioural problems' (Larson and Meehan, 2011: 188). Roy, discussed earlier in this chapter, freely identified violence as the reason for his family breakdown. However, he did not suggest that his use of weed might have been the cause of his going 'crazy' or that he might have had some emotional instability when he attacked his father. Tony, described at the start of this chapter, had, like the participants in Andreou's study of adolescent homelessness, 'suffered early emotional deprivation' (Andreou, 2000: 71) as a result of parental separation and frequent house moves. In conversation, again like the participants in Andreou's work, he 'spoke in a very lifeless voice, as if it required more energy than he had' (ibid.: 72). However, he too seemed not to recognize that his traumatic life experiences might have psychologically damaged him. Neither young man presented as being in robust mental health, and while both might have benefited from talking to a trained professional, their lack of recognition meant that they did not voluntarily access such support. Although 'homelessness in itself may not *cause* mental health problems it may be related to, or a consequence of, a stressful previous life event which may in turn exacerbate, or eventually trigger, mental health problems' (Bines, 1997: 140; emphasis in original).

The young women in the study seemed to demonstrate a better awareness of mental health problems: Natasha was able to describe how the pressure of her mother's job had resulted in her mother being admitted to hospital.

> Mum ended up getting stressed out by it and ended up on medication and in a psychiatric ward.

Arguments between Natasha and her mother continued when her mother returned home from hospital and finally Natasha decided to leave home.

Sarah described a very complex home situation; the mental health issues of her mother, father, brother and herself interacted to produce an unstable home environment which finally resulted in Sarah being thrown out of her family home.

> I got kicked out of my parents' because of arguments between my parents. It was my dad mainly. As I was getting older I started to question how he was treating my mum and stuff and that was the reason I got kicked out. There was one big argument when he just turned on mum and he told her all the things she does wrong and it's like 'you don't do this, you don't do that, you're terrible'. [Dad] had been off ill for two years before for mental health issues himself. I said things to him because nobody else was, and nobody else had for years, and I got kicked out.
>
> (Sarah)

Sarah went on to explain that her father was very traditional and her mother had given up employment once she had children, but that this contribution to domestic security was not recognized. She described how her parents lived lonely lives with ongoing mental health problems, and had blamed their daughter's homelessness on her anger problems. Sarah explained that her younger brother, who had autism, would not challenge his parents for fear that he might also be thrown out of the family home.

> My brother won't say it to them because he doesn't want to get kicked out himself. My parents have managed to spin it in a way that they believe I didn't get kicked out. At the time I had a chest infection and I was given a steroid injection that made me really angry, and that's what really caused it. They've only said this to give themselves peace of mind I think. They don't have any friends. That's so depressing. If they hadn't met it would be a lot happier.

Lack of parental investment

The young people in this study repeatedly displayed a sense of having been abandoned by parent figures. Sometimes this was caused by their working long hours, at other times the young people had no idea why their parents were absent from the family home. As a result of these extended absences, the young people were not able to develop secure attachments.

> My dad wasn't really a dad because he was always out so I don't see him as a dad because he wasn't really there.
>
> (Natasha)

> I never really spoke to my mum. She was out working. It was my stepdad that looked after me and now my stepdad's the only one I speak to out of my whole family.
>
> (Tom)

As a consequence of their absence the young people's parents did not provide 'warmth and support, ... monitor their children's behaviour [or] engage in inductive reasoning and consistent discipline when infractions occur[red]' (Arthur, 2007: 10). Other research completed in the USA has shown that the families of homeless young people 'score lower on parental warmth, supportiveness and monitoring, and higher on parental rejection' (Nebbitt *et al.*, 2007: 546). Without consistent, caring parental role models young people were left to navigate their way in the world alone.

Other factors contributing to family break-up

Other features mentioned which promoted family break-up, though they were not viewed as major factors, included accommodation and pregnancy.

> I just wanted my own space.
>
> (Claire)

> My mum wanted me to move out because there weren't enough room in the house and I wanted to go because I didn't like it there.
>
> (Dillon)

> When mum found out I was pregnant she wasn't happy but she got over it.
>
> (Karen)

Surprisingly, although financial difficulties are acknowledged to be a persistent 'key factor' in homelessness (Greve, 1997: xi), none of the young people in this study mentioned that money problems had contributed to their homelessness, even though such problems were likely to have been an issue for them.

Conclusion

The young people who took part in this study had all lost a secure base and formed part of a growing cohort of single homeless people. Despite having experienced inadequate, sometimes violent home lives and even when living apart from their birth families, they all still clung to the hope that life could be different and that it was possible to achieve an ideal family life with traditional roles where everyone was happy. When asked what an ideal day would be, Nadine summarized her sense of longing by stating that she would want to be with her mother and father, four brothers, three sisters and grandparents, 'going out to a theme park or something', and Natasha described her ideal future as follows:

> I'd love to have children one day. When I've got my own life sorted out and it's not such a mess and I've got something that I can support my child on, and I've got a nice house to bring a baby up in and everything, and he or she'll have a dad around and that. I want two children, a bigger house and my own business.

Without having benefited personally from successful, stable parenting, or having an understanding of the 'mainstream social capital' (Ravenhill, 2008: 39) needed to achieve stereotyped normality, these young people faced significant challenges in achieving perfect family happiness.

Chapter 7

'You know, try and get back with my family, that's what my plans are': Misplaced family loyalties

Introduction

Despite challenging home events which made family life 'less stable ... less caring ... less predictable' (Allan, 1985: 1) and frequently contributed to the young people's problems, many retained the ideal of the comfort of a nuclear family, a place of safety which would act as 'a haven from the harsh realities of the outside world' (ibid.). In an effort to construct this chimera, some of the young people described how they had tried to mend broken relationships or had reached out to other family members to give them the sense of belonging and close relationships they craved. Although some experienced tensions with siblings created by lack of resources or overcrowding, arguments with brothers or sisters were rarely cited as a reason for leaving. Indeed, a deep sense of loyalty and protection was displayed towards siblings, who often helped to provide some security amid tempestuous home backgrounds.

The experience of 'family' and what this constituted varied across the young people's stories. Frequently when families broke up, the main point of tension was between parents, or those adopting a parental role, and their children, and while many young people sought to repair family relationships, their efforts were frequently confounded by tensions involving non-blood-tie imports, such as new father figures. In this uncertain and challenging environment some young people worked to construct new 'families' of friends they had come to trust and felt they could rely on for future support. However, for numbers of young people these groupings were also unstable as they consisted of other transient groups, which for some only served to continue the cycle of disappointment.

This chapter examines: young people's lived experience of families in comparison with an ideal representation of home life and how they were tied, sometimes reluctantly, to their birth relatives; the ways in which they managed kinship conflict and changes to family structure; the impact of broken family groupings on their lives; and how some of them sought to form new alliances to help them navigate their path through life.

Ideal families

People are social beings, and 'parental figures are both the first and main sources of socialisation, being the most important model for future relationships' (Gallarin and Alonso-Arbiol, 2012: 1,601). For this reason 'it is fundamentally important for children to feel safely attached to at least one significant adult, usually a parent figure' (Harris, 2011: 9). It is this adult who takes responsibility for being the child's first tutor, teaching the child social and practical skills within a caring, safe environment which provides clear boundaries and structure. From this secure base young people cement bonds within their family and develop their understanding 'of fairness and reciprocity (give and take) [as] the cornerstone of relational ethics which encompasses the balance of trustworthiness, justice, loyalty, merit, and entitlement in a reciprocal fashion' (Leibig and Green, 1999: 90). Model, 'psychologically well functioning families' (Delsing *et al.*, 2005: 129) create homes where 'mutual justice and trust is ... learned in the earliest phase of the developing interactions between parents and children' (ibid.). As a result children develop loving bonds to family members who they perceive as deserving recipients of their affections. Confident in immediate domestic relationships, children form new bonds and extend their personal networks beyond core family ties. Assured they will be assisted if they run into difficulties, they try out different ideas through active experimentation and in this way build their understanding of the world; in so doing they form their own unique identity, separate from that of their care-givers.

Abraham Maslow (1943) theorized a hierarchy of developmental needs divided into basic, lower-order deficiency needs and higher-order growth needs. During early child development, parents are responsible for meeting both sets of needs. Maslow claimed that unless their lower-order physiological, safety and belonging needs were met, children could not achieve their higher-order needs of 'esteem and self-actualization' (Noltemeyer *et al.*, 2012: 1862) and would be unable to mature into independent, self-assured adults. He further claimed that 'unmet basic needs' (ibid.) negatively affected individuals' later-life emotional and physical well-being and that they would become bodily and psychologically stunted adults unable to form successful relationships. John Bowlby extended Maslow's work with his theory of attachment, suggesting that problems in adolescence may be linked to lack of 'attention, affection and freedom to develop optimally' (Mooney, 2010: 21) in childhood. He further proposed that 'unresponsive or manipulative parenting contributed to later mental health problems' (ibid.), leading to chaotic lifestyles and associations. For some young people in this study damaging early life events appeared to have had a detrimental impact on their development: they appeared beset by insecurities, distrustful of people generally and hesitant to risk connecting with others for fear of being let down.

Natasha, who lived with her mother, father and sister, described her astonishment at how increasing conflict with her mother seemed first to ambush and then to overtake her, resulting in her leaving the family home to live with her boyfriend while still a teenager. At this time, lacking support from her parents, Natasha turned to other family members and relied on her grandmother to help her through this life-changing transition.

> My nana understands me the most out of everyone because she was brought up similar to me. Me and my mum were always arguing. At 16 I thought I'd still be living at home and everything. I thought my mum and dad would still be together. I never expected it. Never expected to move out and live with someone other than a family member at 15, nearly 16. It's weird.
>
> (Natasha)

Natasha's surprise at living away from her family was typical of most young people in the study, who seemed to have little awareness of the complex interactions and sometimes fragile chemistry of domestic life. Although being a parent of a young child might 'demand more perseverance and continuity' (Gallarin and Alonso-Arbiol, 2012: 1602), 'affection and supervision continue being essential factors' (ibid.) for adolescents, who still require the security of a dependable home base where they can share their discoveries and triumphs as well as their challenges and disappointments, knowing they will be supported rather than ridiculed. The family remains a site of learning where young people can benefit from their parents' knowledge and past experience and feel the excitement of teaching adult carers about new developments as each family member reaffirms their loyalty to and support of the others. Through this mutual exchange, family ties are strengthened in a reciprocal celebration of one another's skills and strengths.

The young people in this study longed to be part of an ideal family with loving, tolerant parents who provided 'cognitively stimulating and emotionally supportive home environments' (Noltemeyer *et al.*, 2012: 1863), a family in which parents prioritized their children's needs above their own, ensuring all basic requirements were met, with at least 'one significant adult who will listen ... but who also offers warnings and wisdom' (Watson, 1999). In such model families, 'social affections [were] deeply formed and unselfishly practiced' (Runkle, 1958: 134); family members made time for one another, openly demonstrating their mutual commitment; and children were valued, and knew they belonged and were wanted. Children did not understand the meaning (or impact) of emotional poverty, or want for material goods. If siblings were present, they acted as surrogate tutors, complementing parental guidance and when necessary being peer confidants. In difficult times, the family came together for the good of the whole, bound 'under an obligation to defend or support' each other (Leibig and Green, 1999: 90) in whatever ways they could. When attacked or threatened by outsiders, the family closed ranks, showing a 'special kind of ... group loyalty' (Runkle, 1958: 133) that focused all efforts on protecting the interests of the group. It was this kind of perfect family that the young people in this research so desperately wanted to be a part of.

Even though Ranjit had been brought up by very controlling parents and had been forced to 'flee due to abuse', which Nebbitt *et al.* (2007: 546) find to be a typical pattern, he felt such strong loyalty to his family that when he was thrown out of his home he assumed blame for abandoning his sister and breaking up the family. While far from an imagined ideal, Ranjit's ties were so powerful that, in an ambivalent way, he looked forward to the day when he could return home and be reunited with other family members.

> Dad's in prison. He was a bad person. I regret they've got no man in the house. I was the only man and my dad's not there. My family force me to do everything. They never want me to make my own choice. It was just them all along. In the future when I get a job and stuff, I'll go back home and tell my mum 'Look, I'm here in front of you, a grown man and you kicked me out'. I'll try and get back with my family, that's what my plans are.
>
> (Ranjit)

After a period of separation during which time his family had the 'opportunity to regroup, restructure, and rest', as Nebbitt *et al.*, (2007: 552) expressed it, at Ranjit's request his key worker visited the family to explore if Ranjit could return. When the key worker had completed appropriate safeguarding checks and confirmed that the family unit was now safe, Ranjit was able to fulfil his wish and return home, and all the family members started to rebuild their lives together.

While many young people in this study could imagine a desired idyll of family life, 'this ontogenetic primacy of justice [was] not reflected' in their lives (Delsing *et al.*, 2005: 129). Most of them lived a far more brutal, immediate existence, resulting in many losing all contact with members of their birth family. These young people's relations were far removed from the idealized family unit, but for a few reconciliation remained an achievable goal.

Changes to family organization and managing internal conflict

Changes to domestic living arrangements often destabilized families and accelerated family breakdown. These changes habitually occurred when other adult members joined the family unit and introduced uncertainty to the home, forcing children to renegotiate boundaries with sequential sets of parent figures and to confront issues of loyalty and choice. These changes often coincided with the onset of adolescence, a recognized difficult time for all young people, which further increased turbulence in the home. Research by the Centre for Social Justice has shown that where 'family structures change again and again, ... this has a particularly negative effect on children. [They] have lower cognitive scores[, ...] are more likely to show disruptive behaviour ... and have a higher likelihood of dropping out of school' (2013: 56). Further, mothers 'who re-partner are less likely to have a good relationship with their child' (ibid., quoting Holmes and Kiernan, 2010: [12]), which removes the opportunity to give ongoing support and guidance.

When faced with adversity, families in this study appeared to lack the coping strategies necessary to positively manage change or the willingness to develop solutions to accommodate their new circumstances. Instead of working to find positive solutions for all family members or trying to keep the family together, they frequently seemed to adopt short-term, reactive responses, insisting that their children should leave the family home. This hasty response, while apparently addressing immediate domestic concerns and removing one of the ingredients of internal conflict, seemed to pay little attention to potential long-term outcomes for either children or parents.

When Natasha's mother formed a new relationship with another adult male, Natasha found the home dynamics significantly altered and she regularly argued with her mother about money, college work, her own choice in boyfriends and her mother's choice of partners. She recounted how, after ongoing conflict, her mother issued a final ultimatum directing Natasha to leave the family home.

> I didn't get on with her boyfriend. So she turned to me and said 'well you either stay here and put up with it or you move out and go and live with your boyfriend', so I did. I'm not really in touch with her now and I don't have anything to do with my dad any more. It's just my nan and granddad.
>
> (Natasha)

At 16 Natasha was a minor and legally still the responsibility of her parents, needing their support and guidance. Unlike in ideal families, in which the needs of children would be placed above those of adults, Natasha's mother appears to have prioritized her relationship with a new partner above that of a continued, stable relationship with her daughter. Consequently, it did not appear to be a difficult decision for her mother to eject Natasha from the family home. Without her mother's support Natasha was reliant on the support of grandparents to help her manage changed circumstances.

Poor mental health of adult carers was another contributory factor in producing major family changes. Both Natasha and Sarah recounted how their parents, who had once been employed in jobs with significant responsibility, experienced progressively worsening mental health, which resulted in them being less able to manage their domestic and professional lives. After ongoing family conflict Sarah's mother gave up work, and while her father continued in his job, both her mother and father were prescribed anti-depressants. Natasha's mother, who had once held a responsible job, also developed mental health problems, and had to leave her employment.

> Mum used to be a manager. Then she ended up getting stressed out by it and ended up on medication, then she ended up in a psychiatric ward. I had to go and live with my nan and granddad for three or four months.
>
> (Natasha)

> Mum used to have friends. When we moved she just got cut off from all her friends and didn't really bother making any more. They're [her mother and father] both on anti-depressants and stuff. I can see why because they're lonely. They don't even like each other.
>
> (Sarah)

Mental health problems put further strain on already fragile relationships, which, though not inevitably, accelerated family break-up.

The impact of failed family groupings for young people

When families break up, children may feel betrayed by their carers and lose confidence in adults who have shown themselves to be fickle in their affections and erratic providers. Breakdown can produce 'both short and long term disadvantages' (Tripp and Cockett, 1998: 105) and there is an increased 'probability of poor outcomes ... among children whose parents separate' (Mooney, Oliver and Smith, 2009: 8). Children from these families are more likely to:

- grow up in poorer housing
- experience behavioural problems
- perform less well in school and gain fewer educational qualifications
- need more medical treatment
- leave school and home when young
- become sexually active, pregnant or a parent at an early age, and
- report more depressive symptoms and higher levels of smoking, drinking and other drug use in adolescence and adulthood.

(Centre for Social Justice, 2013: 53)

The impact on young people's mental health is particularly intense; 'dysfunctional parental styles' (Rohde, 2013: 651) create 'high levels of distress' (Hawthorne *et al.*, 2003: 13), 'higher symptoms of psychopathology' (Rohde, 2013: 651) and later feelings of 'anger, distrust, chaos, and insecurity in relationships' (Gallarin and Alonso-Arbiol, 2012: 1602). Children who were brought up in families where there was 'chronic discord between parents' (Hayatbakhsh *et al.*, 2013: 693) tended to be 'more aggressive and depressed, report more learning difficulties and experience more problems with peers than children from intact families' (ibid.: 694).

When young people became homeless many lost contact with their families and, at a time when continued, reliable support is vital simply for survival, some had no contact with any of their genetic relatives who could help them through complex life transitions. Difficulties created by 'parental separation' (Tripp and Cockett, 1998: 106) may be further aggravated if they occur at 'critical periods' (Hayatbakhsh *et al.*, 2013: 694) such as the onset of adolescence. A 1990s study of homeless people in Nottingham found half 'had not been in contact with members of their family for at least a year' (Bowpitt, 1997: 31). Some of this group had become so removed from their families that they had no idea of their whereabouts or any means of contacting them should they have wished to. The same pattern of deliberate alienation was echoed in this research: most young people had either lost contact with, chosen to dissociate from or had very strained relationships with their birth families. This feeling of severance was keenly felt by many of the young people, who were acutely aware that they were on their own and accountable for all aspects of their lives. Most appreciated that they were not fully equipped to manage this level of responsibility while still very young and had needed to become hardened to cope with life's challenges. This was tragically and succinctly summarized by Natasha.

> There would be times when I'd sit there and think 'I just want to talk to my mum and that'. I suppose I wanted to go back home. I used to talk to my sister [but we] fell out. Everyone's said I've gone through a hell of a lot of stuff for my age. I just get on with it, just put my feelings aside. I suppose I just barge through everything and try and forget some things. I don't want anyone to see I'm quite weak. Sometimes I just feel like crying so I have to stay strong and get on with my own life.
>
> (Natasha)

The damaging effects of parental separation were heightened when fathers ceased to be actively involved in their children's lives. The absence of a reliable male role model was particularly challenging for boys, who were 'at least two or three times more likely to end up in prison than those who had grown up with both parents' (Centre for Social Justice, 2013: 60). In order to fill this void, 'a worrying number' (Peart, 2013: 125) of young men have been drawn towards gangs, where they can find other influential males who can assume the role of fathering and become their new 'extended families' (Umunna, 2007). Tom, who had become a father early (aged 15), described his feelings of disappointment and latent resentment towards his parents for leaving him as a child and his distress at not enjoying a broader network of family support.

> My dad walked out on me. I've always said to myself I'm always going to be better than my parents. I'm a better parent than my mum ever was in her life … I grew up without knowing my grandparents and it ain't a nice thing to do.
>
> (Tom)

In contrast, Darren had maintained contact with his parents and siblings. However, he described how, since becoming homeless, he had substituted his boxing trainer, Rock, as an older male father-figure to help resolve personal worries. Rock offered an appealing male-orientated approach to problem solving which Darren could readily relate to.

> I've been with [Rock] for about a year now. He always said if
> you've got a problem with someone, get them in here and jump in
> the ring with them. Like, drag them in the ring and have a boxing
> match. Just settle it out there, because that's fair enough ain't it?
> I'd do that I would.
>
> (Darren)

Darren also admitted to a disquieting reliance on the advice of what he
described as 'the wrong crowd' of similar-aged male peers who had
encouraged him to engage in such activities as 'theft, GBH, fighting, criminal
damage'. Even though Darren openly admitted to engaging in criminal
activities, he had been fortunate enough to avoid custody, but he had
received 'referral orders, cautions, probation, loads of community service
[and] a tag for months and months'.

Ranjit presented a more insular, abandoned picture of homelessness.
When he was thrown out of his family home, he had maintained some
covert contact with his sister as other family members had deliberately
prevented other contact taking place. This was particularly problematic for
Ranjit who, as an Asian male, felt compromised in speaking to his support
network within the Asian community for fear of tarnishing his family's
reputation.

> I've had no contact with my family except my sister. She doesn't
> want to tell mum. I don't want mum getting violent at her. It's one
> of those things you've just got to keep secret. I've tried getting
> in contact with my family, but they've blocked me off from
> everything, like Facebook. Any formal contact, they just block
> me so I can't get back to them. It makes me feel awful, like I need
> to cry my eyes out all the time.
>
> (Ranjit)

Since being accommodated in a housing project, Ranjit had developed a
separate network of support outside of the Asian community and had found
new friends who had the 'same kind of story' as him. He was able to talk
freely to these friends and felt comfortable knowing they shared a common
bond, and Roy, who lived in the same accommodation block and had also
experienced violence in his home life, had become Ranjit's best friend.

Building new families

Without the support of their birth families, the young people actively sought
out 'real friends' (Allan, 1989: 104) who they believed would provide the

consistent encouragement their families had failed to offer, or set about building their own families either with or without the support of a partner. For a few young men this meant electing to 'become part of a gang' (Peart, 2013: 82) that could offer male companionship and physical protection from outside threats.

Consistently with research on broken families completed by the Centre for Social Justice (2013), Tom had become a parent while still a teenager. Once he had recovered from the initial shock of discovering he was to be a father he was determined to take his responsibilities seriously. Even though he separated from his girlfriend during her pregnancy Tom saw his daughter, Eleanor, every week and wanted to do all he could to be a supportive father.

> When I found out, I just remember sitting at the table and smoking loads of fags because I was shocked. I was mad, absolutely mad. I just wanted to walk out of there. Stand up, walk out and keep on walking. Honestly, to this day I don't know what stopped me because I really did want to. But you can't, can you? My dad's done it to me, so I wouldn't. I didn't want that for Eleanor. [Dads] provide food, clothes, money. As soon as I get a job, I can do it.
>
> (Tom)

Tom was proud that Eleanor recognized him as her father, called him 'dada' and physically looked like him. Despite separating from his girlfriend Tom was clear that he should not be replaced by other men and should be the only father to his daughter.

> My sister got two blokes trying to be a dad to her. I didn't want that for Eleanor. Fair enough if she [his ex-girlfriend] gets another boyfriend or something like that, but I wouldn't expect him to act like a father to her because she's already got one. She doesn't need another dad.
>
> (Tom)

Like Tom, Chardonnay and Bella had become parents as teenagers, and while not living with their boyfriends both young women remained in contact with their children's fathers. Similarly, while not full-time fathers these young men continued to play a role in their children's lives, offering some support to Bella and Chardonnay with domestic tasks like feeding and changing.

In contrast, Darren did not try and build himself a traditional family, preferring the camaraderie of male friends who he felt could and would offer protection against outsiders if needed.

> Two people are my best mates. They've always been there for me. If I had a fight and there was loads of them, they would jump in, even if they know full well they were going to get their heads kicked in. They're like my brothers. I chill with mainly them two and about six or seven other people. But I can make one phone call and there'll be about 50 of us.
>
> (Darren)

Even though Darren's friends introduced him to cannabis when he was 13, encouraged him to engage in other illegal activities and appeared to be what Pahl (2000: 161) calls 'dangerous and disruptive' associates, Darren valued and was firmly committed to this group of friends, believing they could be 'relied on to help each other out in times of trouble' (Allan, 1989: 104).

Birth family relationships that had not completely deteriorated were supplemented with support provided by the staff based at the housing project and other support workers, as illustrated by John and Ray.

> I'm pretty much happy because I've got like the family of the Foyer and then my own. I've still got the support worker who helps me who I can talk to. I've moved on and I've still got contact with them.
>
> (John)

> I've got Kayleigh. She's like my mum. Looks after me. Tells me when I'm being a knobhead and being naughty. She does my washing. She irons my clothes. If I've got too much [money] and don't want to look after it myself I give it to her. She helps paying bills. She helps me find out stuff I need to know.
>
> (Ray)

Conclusion

All the young people in this study wanted to be part of a group in which they were valued and recognized, and felt safe and secure. They wanted to be loved and to give love in return. Without ties they were uncertain of their position and seemed at odds with the world around them. They keenly felt the need to be connected with others and to have a base where they knew they would always belong. For some this meant not giving up hope that contact with their birth families could be restored, and some young people did all they could to preserve communication channels when they moved away from their birth parents. This sometimes meant maintaining clandestine contact with siblings. In several cases, grandparents played a significant role in providing shelter and guidance and maintaining the possibility of speaking with parents at a future point. For others, the break-up was felt so intensely that any hope of renewing relations with birth parents had completely disappeared.

When all hope of being reunited was lost, young people sought to re-establish their roles and tried to establish a sense of permanency by building new relationships. Sometimes this meant finding a partner and constructing a traditional family unit of a mother, a father and children. However, none of the young people lived with their partners on a permanent basis; they effectively replicated their own life histories of living with a single parent, and so repeated the cycle of poverty and marginalization. Other young people seemed to have lost confidence in the value of having a partner and did not appear to want to either take the risk or invest the emotional energy needed to form a long-term relationship; instead they reconciled themselves to the company of close platonic friends. One young person appeared so damaged by his life experiences that he seemed resigned to living alone. He summarized his feelings about family and friends in the following way:

> I don't wish for anything because I've never got anything I've wished for, I feel there's no point.
>
> (Tony)

Chapter 8

'If I want something, I'll make sure I get it no matter what': The development of personal resilience

Introduction

This chapter presents the belief that some of the participants had in their ability to bring about change in their lives. In the persistent turmoil of their disorganized lives, many of the young people learnt that there were few people they could rely on; they often had to cope with difficult situations almost entirely alone. As a consequence some of them appeared prematurely aged, or developed a hard single-mindedness not normally associated with youth.

It is evident from the young people's stories that their resilience was a requirement if they were to survive their challenging circumstances. The effect of this resilience is found in their determination to make positive life changes for themselves, or for their own children if they had any. While all were concerned with financial security, the subtext for most of the young people appeared to be the need to build a secure emotional platform from which they could form lasting (and loving) relationships. Although on the surface most of the group appeared hardened by life experiences, this façade seemed to thinly mask an underlying fragile personal disposition created by repeated disappointments, so that they no longer knew whom they could trust. These disappointments led the young people to turn to their own resources to make decisions about their futures.

Developing resilience

> Most of us imagine the family as a place of safety, closeness, intimacy; a place where we can comfortably belong and be accepted just as we are ... yet we know quite well in real life matters are rarely quite so simple.

> (Kuhn, 2002: 1)

It is evident from all of the young people's narratives that family was not considered to be a place of safety, closeness or intimacy. Instead, the young people in this study had to find ways of coping with challenging circumstances not only to secure their immediate safety but also to pave the way for their futures.

Tom showed high levels of maturity when he heard that his girlfriend at the time was pregnant. His reaction, just three months before the birth, illustrates the tension he felt from wanting to run away from the situation, but also accepting his responsibilities towards his unborn child:

> I don't know. Honestly to this day, I don't know what didn't stop me from getting up and walking out that room because I really did want to. Like you know when you've just an urge to do something, like one of them urges, say you're sitting on the sofa and there's a little spot on the telly and you just need to get it off like that, that kind of urge, like you can just feel it, like you just want to get up and walk out and that's how I felt, but I don't know, you can't can you?
>
> (Tom)

While it is generally acknowledged that people tend to adopt a 'fight or flight' (Taylor *et al.*, 2000) response when placed in stressful situations, Tom deals with this shock by freezing. He later goes on to explain how he wanted to be there for his daughter in ways that he felt his parents had not been for him. Tom's change in approach to dealing with stressful situations is clearly evident. When faced with a difficult situation at home, Tom opted for the flight response, stating,

> [m]y stepmum was like 'it's either Tom or me that goes'. And I said, 'well I'll just go then'. Do you know what I mean? Went and moved in with my sister, sister who had really bad depression and like obviously I was looking after her more than she was looking after me.

In this account, Tom illustrates his strength of character in moving out of his family home in order to secure his father's relationship with his stepmother. In addition, he takes on a caring role for his depressed sister, despite his own emotional turmoil at the time. Tom also had a troubled relationship with his stepfather but recognized his own part in the breakdown of this relationship:

> I argued with him [stepdad] all the time, but that was because I was blaming him at the time, but now I've grown up, like I have had to grow up quick. I reckon my sister and me are a little bit like, not messed up, but like we've had to grow up quicker and I don't know why, it's just how it happened.
>
> (Tom)

Tom appreciates that his experiences forced him to grow up quickly. In doing so, he demonstrated high levels of resilience and self-reliance at a young age. For example, Tom was 14 when he was kicked out:

> It was during the summer holidays, so I went and moved in with my mate for six weeks and then went to [place] with my dad.

Tom articulates his chaotic background in a very matter-of-fact way. Such emotional detachment is not unusual in adolescents from troubled backgrounds (Turner *et al.*, 1991). There is a sense in which his experiences have toughened him; he does not display any emotional connection to what has happened and places an emphasis on his need to rely on himself. This comes through strongly as he talks about his plans:

> I just feel like I'm doing something and I'm earning money, like, I'd rather be out there earning money than, I know it like sounds a bit horrible, but sitting here on benefits going to college. If I had time to go to college, I'd be living with my parents still, do you know what I mean? That's when you have time to go to college, but I've not, I've got to look after myself, no one else is going to look after me. So I've got to get a job and get out of here, because while I'm in here, I can't get a job because of the rent situation, but after this course, hopefully I'll be able to get a move-on report, move out and get a job instead of being at college, because I'd rather work than be at college.
>
> (Tom)

A move-on report is constructed when the NCHA believes that everything is in place to support a successful transition into independent living.

Tom has to rely on his own abilities to sort his situation out as he does not have a family support structure to help him. Having a supportive family is recognized as providing the foundations of emotional stability required for successful development into adulthood (Doherty and Hughes, 2009).

Natasha also shows strength of character when faced with a similar ultimatum to Tom's:

> So she turned round to me and she said, 'well you either stay here and you put up with it and you get on with [her partner], or you move out and go and live with your boyfriend'. So I did.
>
> (Natasha)

Natasha also highlights how her being 'kicked out' at a young age had interrupted her expected life trajectory (Byrom and Lightfoot, 2013) and had taken her by surprise:

> Strange, at 16, I thought I'd still be living at home and everything, and I thought my mum and dad would still be together. I never expected it, never expected to move out and live with someone other than a family member at well, 15, nearly 16, it's weird.
>
> (Natasha)

Both Tom and Natasha preferred being homeless to living in what had become untenable situations in their home lives. This is similar to the findings of other research that explored contexts surrounding homelessness, where '[p]articipants commonly described their previous living situation as untenable' (Holtrop *et al.*, 2015: 184). Natasha appeared to move from one untenable situation to another. She moved to her boyfriend's house into what emerged as an abusive relationship. Despite her toughened veneer, Natasha exposed a vulnerability as she described how she was dealing with her current situation and a forthcoming court case against her boyfriend:

> I don't know. Everyone's always asked me that and they said I've gone through a hell of a lot of stuff for my age. I don't know. I just get on with it, just put my feelings aside. I don't know how to describe it. I suppose I just barge through everything and try and forget some things … I think it's, I don't want anyone to see that I'm quite weak … sometimes I just feel like crying and if I don't do things a certain way … thinking 'oh everyone's watching me fail', so I have to stay strong and have to get on with my own life.
>
> (Natasha)

Similarly to Tom, Natasha is battling with an internal tension between what she knows she should do and what she wants to do. This is evident in her most recent discussion with the police:

> When I rang the police the other day, I turned round and I was
> just like 'can I not just drop this now?' When they came out and
> they started talking to me, I kept on thinking it's just going to
> make everything worse, but I've done it now, I need to stick to it.
>
> (Natasha)

As she speaks, there is a sense that Natasha is trying to convince herself to follow the court case through. It is also evident that Natasha is in regular contact with the police, who are providing the support required to enable her to continue with the case. Her emerging resilience is extremely fragile and it is only when the threat comes closer to her current home that the reality of her situation provides her with the incentive to continue:

> It's going through because I had the police out the other day and
> I think it should be getting, he'll be getting done for domestic
> I think and threats, because he were threatening to burn down
> the flat.
>
> (Natasha)

Natasha seems to have normalized abusive behaviour and was willing to drop this aspect of the case against her boyfriend. The threat to burn down the flat brought home the reality of the danger she was in and her need to gain closure and move on. She explains:

> I just thought it's wrecking my life, my life's pretty much wrecked
> as it is, don't need it wrecking any more, I don't know … I think, I
> just think about what I could have in the future if I actually tried
> and applied myself to something.

Literature highlights the role determination and hard work play in transforming life chances (Newman and Blackburn, 2002). Jacob demonstrated his capacity for hard work, high levels of determination and his self-reliance in securing change:

> It's by myself. I didn't have other people helping me achieve
> this goal, it was me who was doing it. I've done it since I was a
> young lad, well about five, started then and then when I was in
> secondary I've started doing my cooking … I've achieved what
> I've done, it's made me pleased with myself, like happy.
>
> (Jacob)

Jacob developed a sense of accomplishment by completing a cookery course. He was unable to commit to a career as a chef, because it had not come to fruition for him yet. He was finding it difficult to secure a job in this area because there were too few available. He was therefore looking for other forms of employment at the time of our interview.

Developing perseverance and getting what I want

It is evident that the young people in this study faced serious challenges and were attempting to turn their lives around through the support of the NCHA. Despite their damaged relationships with parents, they continued to be hopeful that those relationships would be repaired. In Chapter 9 we make reference to how their imagined futures comprised loving family relationships. In their 'fast lane to adulthood' (Wilkinson and Pickett, 2010: 125), the young people in this study demonstrated a strength of character not usually associated with those who have experienced such turbulent times. Natasha, for example, states,

> Yeah, I'm not the type of person to back down until I've won the argument … I think if I want something I make sure I get it no matter what, if that makes any sense?

It was particularly evident as she talked that many of her arguments at home were caused by financial considerations. Interestingly, this was due not to a lack of money, but to Natasha's expectations of how much she would be entitled to. She remembered that most of her arguments with her mother had been about money:

> It sort of reminded me of when I was younger and like when my mum used to have a lot of money and I thought as soon as the divorce money comes through I'll get a car out of it … when I know that someone's got money, like my mum or something, I will pester until I get what I want.
>
> (Natasha)

In line with other studies (see for example Holtrop *et al.*, 2015), we found that, despite the very real challenges the young people in this study experienced, they displayed high levels of perseverance. Natasha had 'gone back to college to finish off my hairdressing course and everything'. Natasha had secured an apprenticeship, which had fallen through. Despite this setback, she had pursued an alternative. She explains:

> Then I found another one [an apprenticeship] and then they said they couldn't afford to keep me on, so then I ended up at college,

which I didn't really want because I know that I don't normally do colleges, but it's worked out so far.

As detailed in Chapter 5, Natasha's experiences of education had not been positive. Her new resolve to engage with education is indicative of her determination to secure an improved future for herself.

Richard found himself in a situation where he was forced to rely on his own resources to sort out his situation. He describes how he experiences 'ups and downs' with little direct support from his parents:

> I've tried sometimes when I have my ups and downs, but I've had advice from my parents saying, you have to get through it, I know it's going to be hard, but you have to get through it, so I was like, fair enough, do something on my own, see where it gets me and it has got me quite far where I am now so –
>
> (Richard)

Limited parental support and intervention are consistent features across the sample. Sarah struggled to gain respect from her family. While she demonstrated strength of character in addressing what she saw as the poor treatment of her mother, her family relationships continued to be problematic until she had moved out. Sarah's determination and perseverance in sorting out her situation had eventually gained her parents' respect and she felt their attitude towards her change:

> No they don't, they treat me like an adult which I like. I like being treated like that because I am living independently now, you know I've proved that I can do it so there's not really any reason why anyone should treat me like a kid any more.
>
> (Sarah)

Enveloping her need to be treated as an adult was Sarah's willingness to challenge her father. She explains:

> Increasing arguments between my parents, it was basically, I started realizing that a lot of the stuff that had, it was my dad mainly like, I don't know, when you're brought up in a house that it's always been like that, you don't question a lot of it, but as I was getting older I started to question like how he was treating my mum and stuff and that was the reason basically, that I got kicked out … I said things to him because nobody else was and nobody else had for years, so it was just like, yeah.
>
> (Sarah)

Sarah knew that challenging her father would result in a very difficult situation, and yet she was prepared to invest emotional time and effort into articulating her views. To some extent Sarah's approach to dealing with her troubled family life is interpreted by her family as exacerbating the problem. She states that her mother and father are 'the sort of people that, if there's a lot of problems they just ignore them'. In this context, and by negating their role in the situation, Sarah's parents bring to life Bauman's criticism of an individualized society:

> In our 'society of individuals' all the messes into which one can get are assumed to be self-made and all the hot water into which one can fall is proclaimed to have been boiled by the hapless failures who have fallen into it.
>
> (Bauman, 2001: 9)

Sarah's parents held the view that she was to blame for the situation and that their lives would be improved if she, as the creator of the 'mess', left the family home. Sarah had achieved what she wanted to achieve and had alerted her father to the inappropriateness of his behaviour towards her mother. While this had cost her place in the family home, she knew that she had done what she considered to be the right thing. In doing so, she had placed herself in a vulnerable situation and in need of support.

Needing interventions

Key workers play an important role in helping homeless young people back into education or employment. The relationship that the young person has with their key worker is therefore key in securing future moves and is possibly the first stable relationship the young person has experienced. Ferguson *et al.* emphasize the importance of the relationships between homeless young people and their key workers:

> The relationships that homeless youth form with service providers within drop-in centers, shelters and transitional living programs are often the first positive experiences these youth encounter with adult role models.
>
> (Ferguson *et al.*, 2011: 1)

Natasha's narrative illustrated her need for intervention from her support worker to prompt her into planning for her future, but also the complexity of the relationship: she did not want the support worker to get angry with her:

> She'll go through it with me, but she'll tell me to do it and then
> most of the time I won't do it and then she'll tell me again and I
> will do it, because I don't want her to get angry with me … I do
> it for me as well, but it just takes a bit of a while.

> (Natasha)

Natasha has experiences of challenging relationships both with her parents
and with her boyfriend. She clearly does not want another turbulent
relationship with her key worker, although she does tend to push the
boundaries by not acting on advice as soon as it is provided. Her need for
continued intervention is illustrated by her frequent communication with
the police but also by the advice she receives from her key worker in relation
to her boyfriend. She acknowledges the support provided by saying,

> I think it's influencing me to get on with my life and that and
> realize no matter what I say and what I think in my head or in my
> heart, that [my partner] ain't good for me. I can get a lot better
> than him and that I can do a lot better with my life now I'm not
> with him and that I can get a good job

> (Natasha)

She appears to need continued reassurances that the relationship is not
positive for her and that she is doing the right thing in progressing with
the court case. She categorically states, '[I deserve] someone a lot better
than him, he's a waste of space', but there is a sense in which she is trying
to convince herself of this position. Literature highlights the importance
of recognizing 'strengths and positive adaptation' (Masten, 2011: 493)
following intervention. Most young people in this study had developed
mechanisms to cope with their situations and were making positive steps
towards a different future, despite their difficulties in trusting others. Sarah,
for example, found it difficult to go through her troubled past with those
who could support her:

> It was soon after [I got kicked out], the person I was living with
> was like 'well I think you should probably go and get that sorted',
> because I'd been as a recommendation to go to see this unit like
> four times and just like cancelled on them, so I was like 'oh no,
> I'm fine, I swear, okay, I'm not going to go' … because I didn't
> want to have to talk through any of my issues with a stranger,
> that was my biggest concern and that doesn't really bother me

now because I'm talking to you two; I've had to talk through quite a lot of things with people since being moved.

(Sarah)

Trusting others was a consistent theme across the sample, and yet trusting others was a key element in being able to reconcile a troubled past. While most of the sample were able to respond positively to their new contexts and begin to evidence self-reliance and resilience, not all the young people could. In the next section we draw attention to Richard and Nicole, who both displayed high levels of dependency on the adults who were involved with them at the time of the interview.

Being reliant on others

Richard's narrative detailed how reliant he was on a small number of individuals who supported him with day-to-day living. When asked what would happen if all the support was removed, he replied:

> I dunno, I'd be a bit fucked wouldn't I? My washing, obviously I wouldn't be able to do my own washing would I? I'd have to learn. Can't really try it very well. I don't know, where would I put all my money? I'd have to find somewhere else to put it … I do a bit of cooking, have some toast and that … well, if I make, just learn how to make microwave meals …yeah … that's what you've got a girlfriend for innit? She'll do the cooking.

(Richard)

It is evident that in Richard's hegemonic view there are gendered roles in society. Since becoming homeless and living at the NCHA, he had a support network of females, including his girlfriend. His girlfriend's mother was instrumental in providing support in many areas of Richard's chaotic life, as the following quote illustrates:

> To be fair I get on with Sophie's mum quite well, she used to take me to court all the time, she's alright, she's done quite a bit for me … Obviously I couldn't do without her because she does help, but obviously … [if she wasn't to] help any more, then obviously I'll put up and shut up … she helps paying bills, she helps me find out stuff that I need to know … like helps me find a flat, she helps me reading the letters, I dunno, does a lot.

(Richard)

Seeking social support has been identified as a mechanism by which homeless young people deal with their situation (Dalton and Pakenham, 2002). Richard seeks this support frequently and does not currently have the personal resources to deal with his circumstances by himself. In addition, he states 'ain't got a plan, just take it as it comes', which further emphasizes his need to live in the present and not think ahead.

Nicole also demonstrated high levels of reliance on her key worker. She was unable to think too far ahead and reluctant to invest time in doing so. When asked what her plans were, she replied 'I don't know'. However, there was an immediate need for her to put some thought into her next steps as her tenancy was due to end in three or four months' time (at the point of the interview). She did indicate that she had been saving for this eventuality, and did not seem overly concerned about the prospect of moving out of her current accommodation:

> [I'm saving] for the important things I need ... if I move out of here I'll have to get furniture and things, that's what will have to be soon ... about three/four months ... I'm not worried. I'll soon like sort myself out.
>
> (Nicole)

As we spoke with Nicole, it became evident that her key worker was supporting her efforts to secure a job. Nicole lacked confidence in herself as a result of her troubled family background and bullying experienced at school. Losing confidence is not unusual for individuals who have experienced such backgrounds (Gilligan, 1999; Newman and Blackburn, 2002) and Nicole was making very good progress in rebuilding her confidence. Once the interview had concluded, Nicole's key worker said that her interview had been extremely positive and she had 'spoken the most [she] had heard from her'.

Jacob relied on advice from others, but not in the same way as Richard and Nicole. He would take on others' advice if he felt he had been listened to, as he explains:

> When I think mostly, it's like fifty-fifty. It's like if I speak to someone about like college or if I'm in college I talk to them about it and if they listen and if they give me good advice then I can take that on, but if they give me not good advice or they don't listen, then I do a different way of helping myself. So there's, it's like fifty-fifty.
>
> (Jacob)

Sarah also explained her dependency on others and said that she had been caught up in a relationship for some time before realizing she had the strength to make decisions for herself:

> I was with someone else for ten months once and I remember just the, I realized that I wasn't even like liking him really, I was with him just because I didn't want to be on my own, and when I realized that, I dumped him.
>
> (Sarah)

It was evident from the data that the young people were developing their levels of resilience and self-reliance as they engaged with their key workers. Some were able to adapt to this new sense of strength and identity more easily than others, the latter case being exemplified by Richard's apparent difficulties with managing relatively basic elements of day-to-day life. Sarah, however, thrived in an environment which had provided an escape from her father. With this new sense of freedom, she was developing the strength to determine which choices and decisions would benefit her.

Conclusion

Many of the young people in this study saw themselves as self-reliant and able to resolve the challenging situations they found themselves in. They believed that the problems they had experienced and continued to face could, in the end, be dealt with. However, their narratives also exposed the very real need they had for the support and intervention of their key workers, who advised them on a range of life skills, including managing their finances, negotiating re-entry into education, liaison with other critical services and their drug usage, as appropriate. While it was important for the young people to develop resilience and perseverance, they continued to have the safety net of their key worker should elements of their life begin to fall apart. Relying on the support and intervention of others is a critical component of whether the young people could begin to take small steps in repairing the damage done to them. Gilligan (1999: 187) acknowledges that 'achieving improvement in some parts of a young person's life may have important positive spill-over effects into other parts'. It is evident that the NCHA provides the appropriate level of resources to support young people making the first steps towards positive change.

Chapter 9

'A decent boyfriend, nice family, nice house and everything – just like all the normal stuff': Aspirations for the future

Introduction

This chapter will focus on the ways in which the young people constructed a framework to enable them to accrue capital for their own progression. They recognized and accepted the need for education in order to bring about change in their lives. This firmly located them in broader societal constructs where educational credentials are valued as symbolic capital – as a passport to improved life chances. Their aspirations traversed both education and personal factors: in describing how they envisaged their futures they also indicated their desire to create a nuclear family. Their future 'perfect' family life was devoid of tension, arguments, financial difficulties and all the other aspects of their current chaotic existence. This idealized construction was resistant to challenge, illustrating how much distance from their current circumstances they desired.

Developing aspirations

Reproduction of social class position is frequently identified as an intransigent issue (see for example Wedge and Prosser, 1973; Webb *et al.*, 2002; Byrom, 2016). Young people who go against the grain of family traditions and aspire to an alternative lifestyle invariably do so as a means to achieve improved life chances (Byrom, 2016). Aspiration setting is a classed experience (Riddell, 2010) and the majority of young people in this study did not have the types of 'proactive parents' (ibid.: 41) that could support educational aspirations. Despite this, Chardonnay pictured her future self 'hopefully at university doing this nursing thing'. Her narrative is fraught with uncertainty: as the first in her immediate family to go to university, she did not have access to anyone who would be able to talk with her about their experiences.

Chardonnay's desire to go to university and become a nurse was influenced by some significant health issues experienced by her siblings: one of her younger brothers had died; another brother had serious health issues and had been hospitalized for some time; her sister had recently experienced a period of illness. Chardonnay wanted to 'work in a hospital with poorly babies' and to date had not been able to realize this aspiration. Hodkinson (2008) argues that decision making is framed by occupational and social structures which are not 'simply the external context within which such decisions are made' (4)

Chardonnay did not know how she could achieve her aspirations. Her view of her future self had been framed by the promise of success gained as a result of the expansion of education, a system that can result in bitter disappointment (Platt, 2011) depending on social class. Also fuelling Chardonnay's aspiration to become a nurse was her deep-felt need to provide a better life for her son:

> Loads of money [to] build a good life for Henry. I will have a job so I will be able to get more money. Ermmm, getting him stuff that he wants like be able to save money so he can go to university.
>
> (Chardonnay)

There is a sense in which Chardonnay is attempting to break cycles of disadvantage through her own career plans and aspirations. Despite endeavours to provide educational opportunities as a route out of poverty, the socio-economic status of young people tends to mirror that of their parents (Cassidy and Lynn, 1991; Byrom, 2016).

Darren also had aspirations for his future, but was not in a position to realize them at the time of the interview. Reflecting on his current situation, Darren knew that he would have to make some life changes in order to fulfil his dream of becoming a boxing teacher. However, he knew that he was not yet ready to make those changes:

> I've had loads of different boxing tutors and they've all said that I'm good, carry it on, but I keep fucking it up by taking drugs and that again … I don't know – I'm still young aren't I? It's not just that I've been taking drugs and drinking, it's smoking as well. I wouldn't want to do it if I'm smoking fags as well, I want to quit everything. So, I'm just going to wait until I've done that,

quit everything, get a decent job and do it like on a Sunday, or Saturday, teach 10 to 16-year-olds.

(Darren)

The lure of taking drugs and involvement with fighting (informal street brawling rather than formal boxing) outweighed the desire to make any move towards securing an improved future. Darren recognized that he needed to address this problem in order to fulfil his aspirations:

> I've calmed down a hell of a lot more. It's just fighting I need to keep away from. I love fighting. I never back down from a fight and the people round here always try it, especially when I'm on my own.

(Darren)

Darren had contacts he looked up to who would be able to support his efforts to secure a job, but he knew that his current lifestyle prohibited them from providing any direct intervention:

> [I'm] trying to find a job but it's hard. He [my friend] doesn't trust me yet, well he trusts me but he doesn't want me to like fuck it up for him if you know what I mean ... he just thinks I need to calm down a bit more, then he's going to help me.

(Darren)

Brooks (2003) identifies the role that friends and peers play in demonstrating what constitutes a feasible choice in relation to higher education. Similar levels of influence play out in Darren's thinking about his future. It is evident from his narrative that he places a weighting on the views of his peer group. In this context, he cannot aspire beyond that which is expected within his group: to do so would isolate him from a network that has proven to be influential and supportive, albeit in relation to his destructive behaviours. The connection he has with this peer group is an element of his imagined future life:

> They're always going to be like there for me. When I do move, they'll be coming to visit. I'll be coming to visit them, probably be down here nearly every weekend anyways, getting bladdered.

(Darren)

In Darren's eyes, getting 'bladdered' and continuing with drug use are an attractive part of Darren's future life. His closest friend has a lifestyle that Darren looks up to and would like to emulate:

> My best mate's brother, the one I always drink with, he's got a
> job, he's got a kid on the way, he's got a nice house, he comes
> out with like just over £400 a week, and he's killing it he is.
> He's smart as well. He smokes cannabis every day, drinks on the
> weekend with us, he's living it. I'd love to have his life.
>
> (Darren)

From Darren's perspective, his friend's brother's life is one to aspire to.
However, Darren acknowledges that he needs to make some changes
in order to move towards this model. Similarly to the young people in
Deuchar's (2009) study, Darren displayed 'a range of quite severe lifestyle
factors which present a greater risk to [his life] than [his] lack of work or
educational engagement' (p. 15). Breaking cycles of dysfunctional lives is
highly problematic and yet, for the young people in this study, it was an
imperative for them to move beyond their current situations.

Bella was a relatively new parent who was unable to conceive of
a future self. In that sense, she was not able to articulate any sense of
aspiration towards education. Her life appeared to be on hold while she
took care of her daughter:

> Well I don't really know what I would say because I'm not there
> yet ... I don't know, because I'm not there yet. I don't know.
> I wouldn't be very happy but I wouldn't know what I would
> say because I'm not there, if you know what I mean. I've not
> really thought about that yet. [I aim to] get a job ... and stuff and
> obviously when Keira is at school and, I don't know.
>
> (Bella)

Sarah's experiences were unusual. Despite her recent slight blip with
education, she had achieved an impressive set of GCSE results. She had
strong ability in maths and had taken both her GCSE and her AS level
early. She secured an A* at GCSE but her AS level had gone badly. She had
been kicked out of the family home while she was studying. Her family
background is more aligned with the values of education than other young
people in the sample. Her father was a paediatric psychologist and her
mother had completed a degree while Sarah was a young child. However,
following a series of serious arguments, she had been kicked out of the
family home. This had not deterred Sarah from her aspiration to go to
university and her future plans, as she explained:

> I plan to complete my A levels. I hope to get good enough grades
> to go to Cambridge Uni, then I hope to, or before that do a

gap year and go like travelling around the world for a bit, do volunteer work ... with my partner ... get a van and just drive around and have fun times.

(Sarah)

Sarah knew that going to Cambridge University was for 'intelligent' people and felt that she had the appropriate academic fit to consider it. She also illustrated her knowledge of the sector and the potential impact of her retaking her AS level maths:

I looked on the website and they said on special circumstances, because they don't like people retaking thing anyway, but I think it is special circumstances, being kicked out, you know, not having a place to live.

(Sarah)

Sarah was able to use her current situation positively to mitigate her academic profile. Sarah came across as confident and determined, although it did become clear that her imagined future self was unclear:

Well, I've changed my mind on a weekly basis on that question for the past like three years – it's not anything this week. This week, I'm enjoying being unemployed and I'm enjoying being a student. Last week was the same actually. I did want to be, at one point, I wanted to go into the Army, then I realized that's really not my thing. I wanted to be a doctor, and I realized I really didn't want to do that either. I wanted to be a chemical engineer, then I tried chemistry at A Level and realized I was terrible. And a marine biologist, that's still like a potential one. That's like, I like the sound of that, going to live on like Australia or Canada as well.

(Sarah)

As the interview progressed, Sarah explained that she was on anti-depressants and was trying to work though some of the issues she faced with her family. Her aspirations were caught up in a complex web of academic success and failure in addition to her need to come to terms with her family history and put it behind her.

Engagement with education is frequently viewed as a route out of poverty (Kemp *et al.*, 2004) and as contributing to processes of social mobility. Education featured in the young people's narratives as a mechanism through which cycles of deprivation could be broken.

Breaking cycles

A history of violence was prevalent within the young people's families. Violence was the main area that would not feature in imagined future lives. Chardonnay recognized the important role she had in ensuring that her child did not engage with violence; 'teaching him not to hit people' was high on her agenda. However, Chardonnay also said that violence is acceptable in certain situations:

> I'm not going to stop him [fighting] but, I'm not that bothered what he does outside of school but obviously I don't want him going on drugs and stuff. But I don't want ... as long as he's got good grades then it's .... It depends though, don't it? Because obviously if someone comes up to him and whacks him I'm not going to expect him to walk away. If he walks away than that's fine but if he hits them I'm not going to go mad about it.

While she does not go into specific details, there is a sense in which fighting and getting into trouble are normalized experiences in her life and therefore she expects that these will feature in her son's despite her desire that they will not: 'I would be really annoyed [if he got involved with the police] because he shouldn't do it'. This projection into the different future is emphasized by her aspirations for her son when she states, 'Henry will not have brothers or sisters. Good grades, going to go to university, going to get a good job.' She further acknowledges the need for Henry to move beyond her own experiences, but recognizes the limitations of her own educational background in this:

> Because I had good reason, This girl told the teachers but they didn't do nothing and then ... so I did it and then yeah – if you've got a good reason then I think it's okay ... because [Henry] shouldn't grow up like me, he should grow up better than me – I've got no grades or nothing, but obviously you can't do the best by your kid if you've got no grades can you?

Making up lost ground and going back into education featured across the entire sample, Chardonnay is not alone in having to repeat English and maths. She comes to this with a different attitude – one that has perhaps been developed through her becoming a mother:

> Yes, I've got to do my English and maths as well there, because I've got no grades, so I've got to do my English and maths there

.... I think that because I want to do it I will try and do it, but in school I didn't want to be there so I didn't try.

It is not unusual for homeless young people to have disrupted education histories (Cameron, McKaig and Taylor, 2003). Getting young people in such circumstances to re-engage with education is highly complex, involving a range of partnerships across the NCHA and local FE providers. Even when young people have been supported back into education and have the desire to gain educational qualifications and break a familial pattern of educational failure, things do not always go smoothly. Darren dropped out of a previous course, explaining:

Apparently, I said it was rubbish and I didn't like it. But I didn't even say that and it started getting all twisted and that and blah, blah, blah. Started saying, 'why did you say this?' I don't like people like … in my ear. It does my head in, so I just like … I'm going. Like 'right don't come back' … I'm going to try and stick to it [this time] and the people there, I don't like them. They're all snobs, silver spoon and everything. Just didn't get along with any of them. They're just completely different to me. [This time will be different] … I'm going to get on with them alright because there's a few people from here and there that are going and the last time I went, I didn't know no one. I had a meeting with her [a college tutor] on Thursday. She said, 'I don't know whether we should bring you back', blah, blah, blah. Yeah I promise to be good ….

A lack of social fit has been identified as a link to working-class failure in education (Wilcox *et al.*, 2005). Darren identified a social difference between himself and others on the course that made him feel uncomfortable and resulted in him dropping out of the course. The process of working out whether they identified with other young people or not influenced the young people's attitudes towards education. They established a sense of otherness in which their own position in social space was determined in relation to that of others (Bourdieu, 1998). The distance or social space between individuals fostered a sense of not belonging. Despite their desires to break the cycle of educational failure, they continued to feel on the margins of a system that privileges middle-class capitals (social, cultural and economic). The young people in this study did not possess the appropriate levels of the various forms of capital (Bourdieu, 1998) to enable them to be successful in compulsory education. While the majority of middle-class pupils enjoy a relatively straightforward journey through education, this is not the case for large numbers of working-class pupils, who experience many barriers to progressing in education (Adonis and Pollard, 1998; Archer, 2003). Darren recognizes the importance of putting aside previous experiences and the value of education in supporting a different future. He stated the following in relation to a course he was about to commence:

> Something to look good on your CV ain't it? Doing that, then once I'm finished that, there's some work experience thing as well that I can pick something and that's it, because I want to work in a warehouse and most warehouse work you need experience, so I want to do some experience in a warehouse, so when I've done that and say if they like me as well, they can just say, 'I like you, you might as well stay and I'll give you this, blah, blah, blah'. They might like me and they might give me a job there and if not, I'll have more chance in getting a job if I've got experience in a warehouse.

Darren had assessed the importance of completing the course, in relation not only to the academic content but also to the prospect of it leading onto a placement. Obtaining real experience in a warehouse was important to him as this was a job that he sought. He saw working in a warehouse as a mechanism through which he could support his desire to become a boxing teacher:

> Boxing. On the side and working in a warehouse bringing in money, that's what I want to do. [You can make money through boxing] if you're really good at it you can, you can become professional and if you become professional you get quite a bit of money for like winning fights, but you have to be really, really good to do that. I don't think I'm that good ... I just ain't got much confidence. I'm not saying I'm not good, but I'm not the best if you know what I mean.

Despite his lack of confidence in himself, Darren continues to articulate his dream of becoming a boxing teacher and supplementing this work with more stable employment in a warehouse. He acknowledges that within his family context, where his 'mum, she sits on her arse on the dole, doesn't do anything. All my family don't do anything really', he would be doing something different. Yet it would appear that his history of education affected his confidence in himself; where he had a very real anxiety about academic failure:

> Yeah – but it might not go the way I want it to go. I could do it all but then it's quite hard to get a job nowadays so if I couldn't get a job then ... [I'm worried] ... Yes and then just going to fail, or I'm going to fail it, like I'm not going to be able to do it.

Previous histories within education were hard to shake off. Darren's sense of self was littered with perceptions of a lack of fit, where other students were 'posh' and had 'silver spoons' and where he lacked the academic ability to succeed. Education for many working-class individuals is viewed as a means of either escape (Overall, 1995) or self-improvement or a mixture of the two (Reay, 2001). Education was not the only way in which the young people in this study wanted to move away from their family histories. Tom, for example, wanted to establish distance between himself as a father and his own experiences as a son:

> My dad's done it to me, like so I wouldn't want, like she [my daughter] didn't choose to be here either. I've always said to myself, I'm always going to be better than what my parents were like, always said it and like now I've actually got a chance to do it, I'm doing it. Do you know mum's always said to me when I was younger, she was like 'You will never understand what it's like to be a parent' and all this lot, and I'm sitting here laughing because, what, a year and six months later, I'm a better parent than she's ever been in her life.

On being probed about what a 'better parent' means, Tom provided insight into how he had frequently been let down by his parents, something he did not wish to repeat as a parent:

> That's one thing I'd definitely do [see my daughter] because my dad's let me down loads of times, so has my mum and it's just not a nice feeling, so I wouldn't let her down like that. Because, it's like, imagine the feeling yeah, of your whole life, like having high hopes all week to see someone and then at the last minute get shot down, like just imagine how excited you are all week for that one day and then bang, like it didn't happen. That's how it was with me pretty much my whole life with my dad, or my mum.

It is evident from the young people's narratives that they wanted to move on from their current situations. This involved re-engagement with education and also some consideration of how they could rectify the mistakes they believed their parents had made. In essence, they wanted to escape and improve themselves in order to create a better future for themselves. However, such escape or self-improvement was influenced by the barriers the young people put in place.

Real and imagined barriers

Future selves were imagined in particular ways. All the young people made reference to increased stability, perhaps recognizing the need to move away from their current chaotic lives. Despite this, there continued to be reasons why action could not be taken immediately: the young people either were not ready, did not know what to consider or were able to lay the blame for not changing elsewhere. Darren, for example, has a range of people advising him to pursue his career of teaching boxing and yet he is not yet ready to do so. He explains:

> My mum's been telling me to do it, my dad's been telling me to do it, my uncle's been telling me to do it, but I want to quit smoking, quit everything before I even start thinking about doing that. I don't want to yet, because I don't want to do anything about it yet, I'm still young. I like doing the stuff I do on the weekends. I enjoy it, why not? I'm still young, you know what I mean?

Darren's reluctance to give up the elements of his life that he enjoys (drinking, taking drugs and fighting) could be the only stability he currently has. He knows what to expect from this lifestyle, and excursions into other lifestyles (e.g. studying) have left him feeling as though he does not fit. Darren also indicates that he is not the instigator of fights and firmly attributes this to the gangs that seem to seek him out:

> I'll try [to stop fighting], but you can't say that ... it's not me that wants to go and fight if you know what I mean. The last time I threw a punch at someone was about a year ago, a year and a half ago, they're the ones that are starting. We just want to get high and get pissed every weekend. These walk about and trying to kick off with everyone, so it's mainly their fault to be honest.

It would appear that Darren's reputation for fighting is supporting his current lifestyle: he is known locally and is sought out because he will rise to the bait. Darren has achieved status and notoriety from this and it is something he is reluctant to relinquish at present.

Dreaming of a better life

Along with the immediate need to gain education qualifications, the young people in this study dreamt of a future that had more stability than what they had experienced. Darren, who had just turned 18, felt that his life would begin at 30 – the point at which he would be settled and holding down a job and teaching boxing. Darren explains that his future life will be as follows:

> I don't know, I reckon in my thirties – I'll have a kid and have a girlfriend and that. Have a nice job and doing the boxing thing I reckon, I think that's what I'll be doing ... I'm hoping it's going to be a lad first. I really want a lad first. But if it was a lad first he's going to be into boxing. I'm telling him he will – he'd be doing boxing with me all the time. But if he wants to go and experiment, like drugs, like doing cannabis, he can go do it, he can experiment, you know what I mean. I ain't a hypocrite. If he wants to do it, if he wants to go and try it and that, then he'd be like blah, blah, blah, you done it, blah, blah, blah.

In highlighting the role he will have with his son, Darren is imagining a close relationship with his son, something he has not experienced with his own father. In addition, his use of drugs has become normalized in his own life and he accepts that his own child could potentially go down this route. The lived and articulated stories of the young people in this study reflected the 'reality of the lives' (Cameron *et al.*, 2003: 11) that were never that far away from crisis or drugs. Natasha was in the process of a court case against her previous partner. She had experienced abuse and was in constant turmoil about whether to proceed with the case or not. She was able to create a vision of stability as she imagined her future life and yet the damaging relationship continued to feature. Natasha imagines her future thus:

> Hopefully I'll have, I might, no, I won't still be living here, I'll be too old then. Hopefully, I'll have like my own, rented out a house and everything, ... my own car, nice like stable job ... probably hairdressing, knowing me ... hopefully married ... knowing my luck it will probably be him [previous boyfriend], two children, probably a bigger house than what I would have had when I

was 20 and probably setting up my own business in hairdressing and beauty … oh and I'll get my dog back.

Despite the need for a disconnection from her current situation, Natasha is unable to conceive of a life without elements of dysfunction, in this case her previous boyfriend. She reiterates her desire for stability and her sense of impending reality:

> I want a nice house, two children, stable relationship and all of that. But then there's part of you that says, knowing my luck it's going to be like this. I think I need to get my head down a bit more, like concentrate a bit more.

Natasha understood that a complete break from her boyfriend was needed, but did not have the strategies or resources to bring that about at the time of the study. Her basic desire for her future was to have 'I don't know, a decent boyfriend, nice family, nice house and everything. I don't know really, just like all the normal stuff and everything I think'.

Darren knew that he would need to leave the place where he was living in order to have a completely fresh start and, importantly, provide that fresh start for his son:

> But when I'm having a kid and family, I'm leaving here, definitely leaving here … just because I'm well known round here, it doesn't mean my son is going to be.

Sarah also makes reference to distance but for very different reasons. She wants to extend her horizons and experience the world:

> Sarah is not a smoker any more, hopefully. Sarah is married. Sarah has a stable job, maybe not, maybe she's travelling around the world and she's just being a bit of a hippy for a while and going to lots of festivals, I don't know. I think that sounds like quite a fun plan for five years, or Sarah's at Uni: Cambridge.

What makes Sarah's narrative of her future life stand out is the use of the third person. While we are not able to read too much into this, it could indicate distance and that Sarah does not quite believe that her imagined future life will be achieved. She goes on to describe the continued difficulties she has with her father and not wanting him to be part of her future, but feeling that this would need to be the case because of tradition rather than what she would want:

> I don't know if I'd want my dad to walk me down the aisle though.
> That's one thing that's, I don't know, it'd just be like urgh. But at
> the same time it's like tradition and stuff. I don't know.

Sarah also acknowledges that her father has been ill and suffered from
mental illness. In accepting this, Sarah attempts to come to terms with his
behaviour towards her, but acknowledges the situation she is in:

> I know, I know, I know. But then sometimes I end up thinking
> like, what if all the times he's been really bad, it's because he's
> really depressed himself. You know, I try and like try and justify
> his behaviour in my head and then I feel bad as well, but it's all a
> bit of an awkward situation.

The idea of a home, a car, children, and in some cases a dog, represented
increased stability for the young people in this study. However, the young
people did struggle to go beyond this level of imagining what their lives
might look like. Jacob summed this up by saying:

> I'm not sure to be honest. It's where myself is now, because
> people say look at yourself in three years' time, but most people
> they haven't got the knowledge or they imagine to see themselves
> in three years' time, it's what they're doing now to get up to
> that three years' time because you don't know what's around
> the corner, you don't know what tomorrow's going to be or a
> month's going to be. So three years, it's a long decision, it's a very
> long – but you have to go from the start, it's like where I am,
> because you said to me like look in three years' time, I was like, I
> don't know where I am in three years' time, I have to get used to
> what I'm doing now and then work my way up.

The immediacy of what the young people faced took priority. They were
able to imagine some sense of stability in their future lives but were unable
to unpick how they would achieve this.

Conclusion

The young people in this study had a range of aspirations that centred on
a stable family life. This is perhaps indicative of the disruption they had
experienced within their own families and the need to imagine an improved
family life. All had understandably been bruised by their experiences and
were learning to cope and deal with the baggage foisted on them by their
experiences. Despite their own lack of family stability, they were able to

fictionalize a future self and life that moved way beyond their childhood experiences. Even if they were not currently able to invest in activities to support their progress towards it, as in Darren's case, they were still able to create a picture of an improved life. Their ability to do this was, in part, a result of the direct interventions provided by the NCHA.

Chapter 10

'Since I've been here I've had a lot of help': The role of housing projects

Introduction

This chapter explores the pivotal role of the housing project and its staff team in helping young people constructively engage with their current realties and begin to build a positive new future. It examines how housing workers were obliged to take on multiple roles, as advocate, counsellor, surrogate parent, legal adviser, financial adviser, benefit counsellor and health worker, while at the same time ensuring that the young people assumed their personal responsibilities of managing their tenancy, maintaining their accommodation and abiding by the housing association rules. This sometimes produced the difficult tension for employees of being both a friend to the young people and a disciplinarian.

The chapter examines how housing projects and staff manage their multiple roles against a backdrop of reduced resources and a political agenda which appears determined to marginalize some groups, such as young people, and exclude them from society. It also considers the personal demands made on project workers as they try to meet the needs – which sometimes conflict – of both the association and of the young people; the needs of the latter are varied and often high-level. While carrying out this multi-faceted role, the team also engaged in more immediate practical support in moments of crisis or risk.

Accommodation options for young people in the UK

Short-term (up to six months) and settled (over six months) accommodation options for homeless young people (excluding institutional accommodation such as secure units, bail hostels, hospitals or custody) in the UK are limited (note that there is no officially agreed definition of short-term and settled accommodation). Broadly speaking, they fall into the five categories listed in Table 10.1. Other options, such as sleeping on the street or squatting in vacant premises, are also possible but usually these are short-term, often measured in days or weeks, and since it was made a criminal offence in 2012 squatting has become much more difficult.

Table 10.1 Main advantages and disadvantages of different forms of accommodation

Type of accommodation	Advantages	Disadvantages
Living rent-free with family or friends	Provided the young person has family or friends, this is usually the most accessible form of accommodation. Sometimes friends (especially boy/girl friends) will accommodate homeless friends or partners. Without the burden of housing costs, young people may be able to save some money. Other 'extras', such as household bills (for example water rates), may be provided. Food may also be included. On-demand non-professional emotional support is often available. Usually safe, particularly if staying with trusted family or friends. This is the preferred, government-encouraged housing option for all young people.	If the accommodation is with friends, more distant family members or part of a 'sofa-surfing' culture, it might only be available for a very short term of a few nights or few weeks. It may be restrictive or controlling. It could be difficult to object to the quality of facilities provided or to make changes to the surroundings. The young person might be made to feel like an outsider.

Type of accommodation	Advantages	Disadvantages
Renting accommodation from family or friends	Lower than market-value rents may be charged, which provides a chance to save money. On a comparable cost/quality basis, this might be better than private-sector housing. The young person may be familiar with the habits and behaviours of the hosts. If the accommodation is with friends, it could be an opportunity to feel part of a family; this might be especially desirable if the young person has previously experienced negative family relationships.	Might be the worst of both worlds, with the competitive pricing of the private sector being coupled with the controlling behaviour of families. It could be hard to criticize the facilities.
Renting from a private landlord or other profit-making organization, including some hostels and bed & breakfast accommodation	Provides one's own space which, within the conditions of the tenancy agreement, can be customized to suit own tastes. Offers a sense of freedom.	Rents could be high as the landlord will be seeking to maximize profits. The landlord may not regularly carry out routine maintenance as they will wish to minimize costs. Renting alone might feel isolating.
Renting from a public landlord, charity or other non-profit-making group, including housing associations and some hostels	The rent and standard of accommodation are likely to be fair and will be regulated. Other support facilities, such as counselling or help with budgeting, may be offered. This could provide the opportunity to network and socialize with others in similar circumstances.	It may be difficult to secure a tenancy as young single people are not classified as a high-priority group and there are often long waiting lists. The choice of type of accommodation will be limited and the young person might be obliged to accept housing in an unattractive area.

Type of accommodation	Advantages	Disadvantages
Buying a property	Gives full control of all aspects of the property. If the property is large enough the owner could let to tenants or lodgers and raise additional income.	Unless the applicant is in a secure, well-paid job it may be hard to obtain a mortgage. Lenders will only lend a proportion of the value of the property, so the buyer needs a large deposit. Mortgages are only available to people over the age of 18. The owner is fully responsible for all aspects of property maintenance.

The work of housing associations in the UK

Housing associations cannot be easily categorized. They are 'neither private trading bodies driven by the profit motive, nor democratically elected public bodies, nor government appointed bodies' (Malpass, 2000a: 3). Their single purpose is to provide 'housing for lower-income groups in housing need' (Mullins, 2000: 256). In 1979, local councils were 'the largest landlords in the country, accounting for 32 per cent of the housing stock of Great Britain' (Balchin and Rhoden, 2002: 136). However, collectively, housing associations are now the principal provider of social housing in the UK.

The roots of housing associations can be traced back to 1830 with the establishment of the 'Labourer's Friendly Society' (Balchin and Rhoden, 2002: 194). Growth in the nineteenth and early twentieth centuries saw the establishment of more associations, including the Guinness Trust, the Peabody Trust and the Joseph Rowntree Trust (JRT), all of which still exist. Most of these groups were based in large metropolitan areas where there was a shortage of accommodation for an expanding industrial workforce. Some associations set up by industrialists like JRT were carefully designed to create optimal living environments providing high-quality housing coupled with good public utilities such as education and health services. Unfortunately, not all associations were well run or well managed and some significantly 'deviated from their original intention to house only the poor' (Malpass, 2000b: 199). This failure brought some associations under close scrutiny and they were obliged to revise their working practices and improve the standard of their properties.

Although early associations intended to meet the accommodation needs of the poorest in society it became increasingly apparent that this goal was not achievable and that 'state help [was] essential for shifting the housing problem' (Gauldie, 1974: 235) created by a rising urban population. While the state initially adopted a laissez-faire attitude to housing, the First World War produced calls for more responsive government and fairer, more regulated housing policies. This led to council-sponsored projects 'developed by local authorities' (Malpass, 2000b: 73) as they 'took on responsibility for providing housing ... for those unable to meet their need ... through the market' (Mullins, 2000: 266). However, despite this growth in council accommodation the private sector, charitable and not-for-profit organizations still provided the bulk of all housing in the early twentieth century. After the Second World War pressure for affordable housing increased; there were public calls for decent homes for returning heroes. The newly elected Labour Government, as part of its commitment to building a new welfare state, encouraged local authorities to undertake 'new building, slum clearance and improvement of older dwellings' (Mullins and Murie, 2008: 344). While housing associations and others continued to play a limited but important role in supplying homes, the government made it clear that it expected local authorities to take the lead in providing social accommodation and as a result 'a million council houses were built in just seven years' (Malpass, 2000a: 121).

However, later governments have taken differing views on the appropriate mix of state-controlled and independently supplied housing, and 'under three Thatcher governments local authorities' share of the total stock fell dramatically' (Balchin and Rhoden, 2002: 136). This decline was further accelerated by the right-to-buy legislation introduced by the Thatcher administration as part of the 1980 Housing Act. Under this Act local authorities were obliged to offer existing council tenants the chance to purchase their homes at significantly less than the market value. With subsidies of up to 50 per cent of the market value, many tenants exercised their right to purchase their homes and to become part of the 'property-owning democracy' (Lowe, 2005: 247). Even greater pressure was placed on available council housing stock as local authorities were prohibited by the Act from investing the income raised into building new homes.

The void created by the sale of council housing has since been filled by housing associations. Many local authorities supported large-scale transfer of their residential property assets to associations, which are now the main supplier of affordable social housing in the UK. In 2017 the UK government recognized over 1700 providers of social housing in England, including housing associations, co-operatives and charitable trusts (GOV. UK, 2017). Many housing associations, such as Peabody and JRT, are now large organizations employing hundreds of staff, controlling thousands of properties with millions of pounds in turnover. The largest associations are based in London and other metropolitan areas but there are also many regional associations meeting local needs.

However, as the associations have picked up the mantle of the nation's landlord they have lost much of the autonomy the once enjoyed and

> their development activity remains heavily dependent upon grant aid, which is distributed largely on the basis of housing strategies formulated by the local authorities; high proportions of new tenants are nominated by local authorities, and most tenants rely on housing benefit to pay their rent. Thus housing associations in the 1990s have a de jure independence but the de facto situation is that they are thoroughly incorporated within the fragmented welfare state.
>
> (Malpass, 2000b: 211)

Nottingham Community Housing Association

The Nottingham Community Housing Association was established in 1973 and is one of the largest providers of social housing in the Midlands, managing over 8,900 properties in six different counties, in locations ranging from inner-city to rural areas. It employs over 1000 staff and has an annual turnover of 62 million pounds. It is guided by a social responsibility agenda and seeks to work with all its stake-holders to provide high-quality, low-cost housing for people in need.

The association provides permanent and short-term transitional housing for single people, families and others. While the association works with anyone needing stable accommodation, it also supports a number of projects for higher-need service users, who include homeless people, vulnerable youth, those with mental health concerns, people with learning disabilities, survivors of domestic violence, teenage parents, older people and Asian elders. The association helps these groups to find homes and, if necessary, provides ongoing support to help service users live independently.

In addition to accommodation the association offers work experience opportunities for people of all ages, including tenants, to help them back into employment, together with an apprenticeship scheme in housing, social care, building trades and business administration. It provides different accredited courses for service users from entry level (pre-GCSE standard), through level-1 (equivalent to GCSE grades D–G) and on to level-2 qualifications (equivalent to GCSE grades A*–C). It offers a wide range of accredited life skill-type topics, including healthy living, stress management, parenting skills, personal money management and peer mentoring. Other, non-accredited training in social skills, personal care and property maintenance is also available. While the association encourages its service users to try to increase their skill sets, it recognizes that further structured study is not appropriate for all tenants. To accommodate this range of different learning needs the association allows residents to participate in programmes solely for the learning experience, should they so choose.

Nottingham Community Housing Association's work with young people

The association works with vulnerable young people aged 16 to 25 across the Midlands, providing supported housing for over 2,000 young people. Some 16- to 25-year-olds can manage their affairs without assistance, but young people who require additional help by virtue of their age, a special need or pregnancy are placed in one of the association's supported housing projects in a short-term let for up to two years. While living in supported housing young people are allocated a named key worker who acts as a central co-ordinating and moral support figure. The worker helps the young person to manage ongoing or arising issues and to plan personalized exit strategies, commonly referred to as 'Move-On options [which offer] help finding housing, making agreements with landlords ... and arranging floating ... supports' (Gaetz and Scott, 2012: 20). This key worker also helps the young person produce a personalized action plan designed to support progress towards an agreed set of goals. These goals can include anything the young person has identified as important, such as anger management, budgeting, re-establishing contact with family members, learning to cook or reducing alcohol consumption. While the key workers' brief is to encourage the young person to make productive decisions, they are obliged to respect confidentiality and the young person's choices. The worker will highlight the risks and potential consequences of any decision, but in the end allows the young person to retain full decision-making control. The only time this working practice is not followed is if there was a safeguarding or criminality issue which could place the young person or others at risk. In this case the key worker would inform appropriate authorities, such as social services or the police, of potential problems. While living in association accommodation the young people are helped to study for further qualifications, volunteer or find employment, and to claim all relevant benefits.

Outside standard working hours, young people are given telephone help by the association's 24-hour support team. This team can give immediate advice on a variety of topics, including minor first aid, can signpost to other agencies, and if necessary can contact emergency services. The 24-hour support team's role is to review the nature of the telephone enquiry and assess whether immediate action is needed or whether, given relevant advice, the issue could wait until later. For example, if the young person had cut themselves and was bleeding profusely the support team would probably telephone for an ambulance, but if the call was about an argument with a boy/girl friend the advice might be to wait until the following day when everyone had calmed down before doing anything at all.

One of the principal ways in which the Nottingham Community Housing Association supports young people is through its provision of foyer accommodation. Foyers, which are 'based on a French model' (Quilgars and Anderson, 1997: 216), operate throughout mainland Europe, Australia, the US and Canada, although the UK and Australia 'have the most expansive system of foyers' (Gaetz and Scott, 2012: 19). Foyers act as bridges from homelessness to permanent stable accommodation and were 'first implemented in Britain in 1992' (ibid.). Even for young people from secure, caring backgrounds the 'transition from childhood to adulthood ... can be challenging and potentially problematic' (ibid.: 8). For homeless young people this transition can become an almost insurmountable obstacle. Their age, inexperience and lack of finances make them prey to 'unscrupulous landlords' (ibid.: 7) and others wishing to exploit their vulnerability. Without a secure base they can return to for guidance they are at risk of further abuse. The foyer model recognizes that many homeless young people are not ready to live completely independent lives and provides a 'safe, supportive environment where residents can overcome trauma, begin to address the issues that led to homelessness or kept them homeless, and begin to rebuild their support network' (CMHC, 2004: 2). Foyers differ from many hostels as they offer 'an integrated approach to meeting the needs of young people during their transition from dependence to independence by linking affordable accommodation to training and employment' (Quilgars and Anderson, 1997: 220). The physical and temporal space provided by foyers gives young people the time to 'grow and learn – and make mistakes – that [is] typically deemed necessary for ... making the transition to adulthood' (Gaetz and Scott, 2012: 10). Expressed simply, foyers give young people a safe place to grow up.

Nottingham Community Housing Association provides extensive foyer accommodation in either self-contained flats or bedsits. All accommodation is fully furnished to a high standard, in recognition that young people may not be able to afford to buy furniture or essential kitchen appliances. Foyers are located either close to or within easy reach of town centres, which ensures access to other services, possible employment opportunities and recreation facilities. Most foyers have some kind of communal area where tenants can meet other residents, personal guests or their key worker, reducing the potential for isolation. Tenants are allowed visitors who can stay overnight for up to three nights. Community involvement is encouraged through regular tenant meetings where the residents meet to discuss the operation of the foyer and make suggestions for improvement. Although there is only limited information, current data suggests that foyers have been successful in helping young people to achieve 'permanent housing … [and] greater reliance on employment rather than income assistance' (Kraus *et al.*, 2007: 38) as well as in assisting 'less skilled young people to compete for existing employment and housing opportunities' (Joseph Rowntree Foundation, 1995: [1]). It thus appears that foyers have been successful in helping numbers of young people navigate a route back into employment and mainstream society.

The role of a housing association worker

Young, homeless people often present a cocktail of multiple concerns, including poor mental health and 'poor education qualifications' (Gaetz, 2012: 7). They are 'more likely [than the general population] to live in relative poverty' and need 'assistance with tasks associated with daily living' (Pleace, 1997: 162) or 'training in daily living skills' (ibid: 167). Nottingham Community Housing Association works with young people to help them address these issues and try and build a better life for themselves. As a consequence association staff have a multi-disciplinary role covering health, education, life skills and employment, and need a good level of competence in each of these areas as well as knowing when to direct young people to appropriate external support. To try and manage these disparate, sometimes unrelated, roles, association staff put young people at the centre of all their work and then consider what service is needed at any given time. Because of the many requirements of their job, workers found it difficult to precisely describe their role and talked about it in the following way:

> You've got to be person-centred. You've got to be a people person. It's trying to look at the whole person in front of you. It's getting [residents] ready for independent living. On the face of it that's what we do but because young people can be slightly chaotic

and some of them have quite high support needs we've got to be a jack of all trades really: mental health, drug and alcohol, domestic violence, learning disabilities.

(Mark, staff member)

When asked what a typical day involved, again staff struggled to explain the principal tasks of a 'normal' day and instead chose to refer to the diversity of their position, maintaining there was no such thing as a usual day.

Every day is a different day and every incident is a different incident. We support young people get back into education, sometimes employment if they want to get back into employment, budgeting, life skills.

(Claire, staff member)

Even though association staff were keen to emphasize the fluidity and diversity of their role, there was a degree of consistency in the type of work covered. Some of the main types of support offered by staff are now discussed.

Personal support

This was the principal activity of all staff. They used a Rogerian (Rogers *et al.*, 2003) philosophy to structure their work with young people. Young people were not seen as problems to be fixed, rather as individuals who found themselves in a particular situation at a defined moment and needed assistance to move forward. Staff saw their role as listening, using their professional experience to assess the nature of need, helping a young person explore options and then planning with the young person how to address the issue. The workers were clear that young people had full control of their personal decisions and staff would not impose other agendas. If a young person was in danger of taking risks, workers would explain possible consequences but would still support the young person with that decision and, similarly to young people living at home, offer follow-up support if disaster struck.

There's a difference between sorting them out and supporting them. You know, push people into your own way of thinking.

(Claire, staff member)

It's like advice and guidance. You can guide them one way, but you can't tell them do something, like 'you do this'.

(Mark, staff member)

> Sometimes the advice we give them would be very strong advice, but we're not going to lock them in their room and not let them leave. We lay it all out in a mature way and then they make that decision. If something happens obviously we're there to pick up the pieces.
>
> (Precious, staff member)

The personal support provided was fluid and could include virtually anything, from accompanying a young person to a difficult appointment (like a court appearance) to taking them to a job interview, or if requested attending as a birth partner.

> Like my first week in the job I was in court.
>
> (Precious, staff member)

> I've never seen a baby born, it would be nice to actually experience that. I would be like 'yeah, I'll go, I'll go'.
>
> (Sacha, staff member)

Education and training support

Often more than half of foyer tenants were classified as not in education, employment or training (NEET). Education is seen as vital in helping young people 'make a success of their lives' (DCSF, 2008: i). Association staff worked with residents to help them access relevant programmes which would enhance their skills and support a route into employment. John described his route into education while living at the foyer and how he was hoping his study would lead to employment:

> I started about two years ago in college and I've done my catering course. I've been thinking what to do with my cooking skills, like get a job, go further.

Association staff were keen to support education and did all they could to help tenants achieve their full academic potential, including helping residents apply for university if they were able to.

> Education is the best option for many reasons. With education you can better yourself, your opportunities are much wider and you can develop yourself. It keeps them busy. If they're not engaging in something, their mental health can deteriorate or because they're bored so they start playing up.

> I used to support this young girl. She went to Manchester University studying social services. She got her qualification, graduated and we did a reference for her to get her own property. She's doing really well. There is quite a few we could tell you about.
>
> (Sacha, staff member)

In contrast, Nadine and Ray had both taken part in the informal learning opportunities arranged by the association. Nadine had learnt basic cookery skills and had worked with other foyer residents to prepare a meal, and Ray had visited a gym to learn about personal fitness and diet.

> We worked as a team. One of us prepared the chicken, a few of us checked it and another one was dishing out. We all took part in it and was all having our own opinions about if it's cooked or not. For chicken you have to make sure it's cooked and not pink.
>
> (Nadine)

> [In the gym] he showed me what to do and that. Told me what to do and stuff. Like what to eat to get bigger and what weights to do and how to do them and that.
>
> (Roy)

While neither Nadine, John nor Ray had secured employment, they had developed new skills which improved the quality of their lives and should help them apply for future job vacancies.

Employment support

Although there 'has always been a proportion of young people who have … been economically inactive' (Peart and Atkins, 2011: 82) successive governments have tried to reduce youth unemployment, albeit by very different means. The Nottingham Community Housing Association works to support young people in their attempts to gain employment when they are ready to make this transition. Sharon (staff) worked extensively with Nadine (tenant) to help her identify employment opportunities by searching through the local newspaper and online adverts. She then helped Nadine apply for a retail sales post and took her to interview to provide moral support and encouragement. Similarly, John was supported with an in-house volunteering opportunity focused on helping him gain a position in catering

I've been doing catering at college and the Tea Club at the Foyer. I've lived here for two years and the support workers give me advice. I can trust them.

(John)

Conflict resolution

The chaotic lives of the young people in foyers sometimes created conflict with other individuals and groups. These situations might arise in foyer accommodation, their parental homes, in education or with members of the general public. The young people did not always have the skills needed to resolve these problems and association staff intervened to help reach a positive outcome. When young people experienced problems with their families, if it was safe the association staff tried to help the young people find solutions to enable them continue living with their families.

> On a daily basis we're there to listen. If it's a family breakdown that could have been resolved instead of him being chucked out we would come in and meet with the family. Obviously we're not there to tell them what to do, we're there to listen and let them find a solution. See if we can get them back together.
>
> (Sacha, staff member)

> We're happy to have them but we'd prefer them to be at home where it is safe, where they're getting that love and that support so we'd encourage them to speak and sort the differences.
>
> (Precious, staff member)

> Every day this young girl was rowing with her mum. She completely smashed her mum's house up. The mum phoned the police. I rang mum because girl came back to the project. She was so upset – 'I've assaulted my mum, she's going to press charges'. I phoned mum. I pleaded with her. I sat the girl down and said 'It's got to stop or you're going to end up in prison.' I really spoke to her.
>
> (Sacha, staff member)

If internal tensions arose between residents, staff would first remind young people of the terms of their tenancy agreement, which required tenants to adopt appropriate standards of behaviour and not to use any form of aggression towards other residents in the property.

> You have to have respect for your neighbours. No noise, anti-social behaviour or anything. We try and get everyone to appreciate what a good neighbour is, not just for other tenants but for people in the community as well.
>
> (Claire, staff member)

However, if tenants did not take personal responsibility for their actions and continued to provoke other residents, staff would intervene to try and broker a solution to the problem or reach a compromise.

> If service users put in grievances against other service users we try and mediate. Try and work it out, find some sort of common ground but sometimes there are big divisions and you can't force it. You just have to try and make sure everyone's safe.
>
> (Mark, staff member)

If it became impossible to resolve matters, eviction would be considered, but this would only be used as a very last resort and after all other avenues had been explored and exhausted.

Budgeting

For many young people living in association accommodation this was their first experience of living independently and they were not competent at budgeting so that their money lasted until their next benefit payment or wage. They needed support to identify essential items and to calculate regular expenditure.

> So when they first come in they score themselves. Can they budget really well? What about their food shopping and their electric and service charge? Sometimes they'll put themselves at 10 for everything and I'll go 'Why are you in supported housing?' Then at the next meeting they'll be more realistic.
>
> (Sacha, staff member)

To help young people look after their money, the association had developed a dedicated, non-accredited three-week financial management course designed to help tenants meet their commitments and stay within budget. Michelle (a tenant), who attended the course, received practical advice on how to shop for the best value, budget and plan for special occasions, understand fuel and energy costs and set up and manage a back account, and on what to do if she fell into debt. After attending the training Michelle was able to speak in the following way:

I was going through a bit of financial difficulties. I went to Better Budgets because my rent was in debt. I didn't understand bills. Better Budgets helped me sort it out. Focus on the things that need sorting right now. I know how to shop and where to shop.

(Michelle)

Jules, another tenant, stated:

Now I'm a million times better off than I was when I first started.

Conclusion

Young people living in association properties had a wide range of needs and project staff worked with tenants to help them find solutions to or ways of managing their varied problems. This sometimes involved having forthright discussions with the residents and explaining to them the risks involved in their behaviour and the extreme consequences that could follow. Young people sometimes repeatedly put themselves in difficult positions and had not necessarily developed the skills needed to disentangle themselves from these complex situations. Project staff themselves needed boundless patience to help them work with young people to try and resolve these issues in a positive way.

Because their role was so diverse, staff had difficulty describing their work. Although they were not the parents of the young person in question, workers often assumed a parental role and were the responsible adults who intervened to resolve matters. The person-centred approach adopted and the ongoing care provided by foyer staff were summarized by Sacha in the following way:

I'm not their mum or their dad, but a really good, positive role model. Someone that's there for them. We're always here as a safety net. If they ever need a bit of advice or support they can come back and we'll support them. You're constantly thinking about work. I've got responsibility. I've got to make sure my tenants are okay.

(Sacha, staff member)

Chapter 11

'Ain't got a plan, just take it as it comes': The role of peer mentoring in supporting homeless young people

Introduction

Intervention from key workers facilitated the young people's re-engagement with education and their capacity to access needed services. While this focus brings about change in the young people's lives, the NCHA also engaged in an innovative programme of intervention: a peer mentoring programme titled Wavelength. Much of the literature on peer mentoring deals with the education field. However, the model of establishing a peer mentoring programme within the housing association was not new to the NCHA.

Built on a successful recent history of providing peer support through the NCHA's innovative Sound as a Pound programme (which provided a point-of-need contact focused on monetary advice and support), the peer mentoring programme was established to offer tenants support across a wide range of areas, moving beyond purely financial confidence building. In addition, the scope of Wavelength included a wider spread of geographical locations across the East Midlands, where the NCHA has supported housing projects.

The wider benefits of being involved in Sound as a Pound included the development of a range of transferable skills and the opportunity to acquire accredited qualifications. From the success of Sound as a Pound (which was focused on Nottingham) and a funding opportunity through the Vulnerable and Disengaged Young People Fund (VDYPF), the NCHA team wanted to expand the ways in which peer support operated to include tenants in the Young Persons Services provision of Housing with Care and Support.

NCHA staff identified a clear set of perceived benefits for mentors attached to involvement with the programme (see Appendices A–C for all the information provided for the recruitment and support of peer mentors). The perceived benefits were constructed as a result of NCHA's experiences with Sound as a Pound. There was evidence to support the proposition that the perceived benefits for both the mentors and the mentees would be transferred to the Wavelength project. This chapter therefore explores the Wavelength project, from its recruitment process to the ways in which both mentors and mentees engaged with it.

Recruitment and training

It is widely recognized that peer mentoring provides a mechanism through which additional layers of support can be provided for those who need it most (see for example Allen *et al.*, 1997; Glaser *et al.*, 2006; Karcher *et al.*, 2006). In addition, it has been noted that mentors themselves gain in a variety of ways from mentoring others (Allen *et al.*, 1997). The NCHA identify 20 benefits of peer mentoring, which were used to recruit mentors onto the programme. Given the positive experience of recruiting onto Sound as a Pound (which attracted 45 peer mentors), there was a clear expectation that a similar number of peer mentors for Wavelength could be recruited. A total of 27 peer mentors were recruited onto the Wavelength programme. This represented 2.7% of the NCHA population at the time of this study. Recruitment was negatively impacted by the transient nature of the population under consideration and the difficulties staff experience in keeping a track on their movements. Staff said that

> more were contacted but they simply fell off the grid and we lost contact with them: some have gone into employment and some of them have been on courses we arranged for them – other training we arranged in-house.
>
> (Sacha, staff member)

Despite the recruitment of 27 young people as mentors, only 15 attended the training. NCHA staff acknowledged that this was a feature of the young people they dealt with.

> some will be agreeable to come on board and then non-committal about the training because they have other things going on – it's not a priority for them. Those who said they would [peer mentor] were unreliable.
>
> (Precious, staff member)

Staff recognized that their recruitment process might have served as a barrier to some young people. Given the demographic composition of the target group, this was not surprising (Greene and Puetzer, 2002). Young people were required to bring in a range of supportive documents, including identification. The tracking of these proved problematic as staffing difficulties across the NCHA became more frequent. The staff acknowledged that they were unable 'to maintain continuity with them [previous tenants] ... and so we were unable to keep contact with them' (Lisa, staff member).

The tracking of tenants and, particularly, former tenants was problematic and contributed to the difficulties the team experienced in ensuring Wavelength's success. The team has already identified areas where improvements could be made to secure the recruitment of more participants on to the peer mentoring programme, particularly in relation to developing a culture in which participation is expected:

> What we recognized was that trying to recruit people who had left was difficult. We need to sort out our side of keeping in contact with them. We are going to build a culture or structure that peer mentoring is something we do. At the point that they come in, that we start working with them on moving on, they will be asked to mentor those who are starting their journey with us.
>
> (John, staff member)

Similarly to other mentoring programmes (Greene and Puetzer, 2002), it was evident through the focus group discussions that peer mentors engaged with a range of training activities to ensure that they were suitably equipped to perform their peer mentoring role. This included awareness of boundaries, of safeguarding issues, of finance, of wider opportunities connected with apprenticeships and gaining qualifications and of the limitations of the role. For example, Louise, a peer mentor, explained that they had 'such a good system where if we don't know the answer we'll refer on and we'll find somebody who does know the answer'. Referring on and appreciating the limitations of the role (Allen *et al.*, 1997) were also mentioned in relation to mentee activities that could be categorized as either safeguarding issues or potentially law-breaking. The mentors were very clear that in such circumstances they would inform the mentee that they would have to pass this information on, usually to staff at the NCHA in the first instance. Louise further stated:

> It's about explaining to that person where we're at and the safeguarding issues ... we'd have to explain to them, look these are the issues, this is what could happen, if you tell me this or if you tell me something like somebody's been hitting you or beating you or abusing you, I'm going to have to report that to so-and-so.

It was very clear from both Louise and Lisa that they had established very clear boundaries around their personal and professional lives. They recognized that inviting a mentee into their home would not be appropriate, for safety reasons but also because of the need to keep their home lives very separate from their peer mentoring role. Louise said:

> I'm not qualified to have a person in my house. I don't know that person. They could seem lovely, but then they could come into my house and steal everything when I went to the toilet, you know it [the meeting] needs to be in a public place. Anybody you invite who's totally unknown to you in your house is a danger.

Lisa added, 'This is work, that is my home, two totally different separate things', underlining her need to ensure that her personal and professional lives are kept distinct from each other.

The training clearly provided information on the process of referral: all enquiries went through the NCHA and were passed on to the peer mentors. Each peer mentor was responsible for informing the NCHA of the details of the meeting, to ensure their safety.

An additional benefit of being involved in the peer mentoring programmes was the gaining of academic qualifications, something that many of the peer mentors had not previously experienced. As detailed in Chapter 5, there is a clear link between living in disadvantage and poor education (Wedge and Prosser, 1973). Achievements for peer mentors included: a National Open College Network Level 2 Award in Peer Mentoring, a role as a teaching assistant, a national award from the National Institute of Adult Continuing Education (NIACE) and an Adult Learners' Week award (two mentors), a one-year administration apprenticeship, attendance at a one-day course in London on how to build a mobile phone app and a regional award for the Most Outstanding Individual.

Lisa emphasizes the impact of the training on her:

> It's taught me so much and increased my knowledge so much to feel even more confident to go out there and help people. I was, like you say, I've not actually done that physically yet, but the training has given me confidence within myself to know that I should be able to go and help people and confident enough to know even if I can't I will go and find where I can get them some help from.

Lisa, despite having received the training, had not yet mentored any of her peers. Of the 27 young people who attended the training, seven had engaged in a number of peer mentoring interactions. Another six young people, who had not been trained as mentors, had been involved in peer mentoring interactions. There is therefore a mismatch between those who are trained and those who go on to peer mentor.

Clarity of roles

All young people housed within the NCHA have access to a support worker along with other channels of targeted support. Understanding roles and responsibilities within a mentoring programme is key to its success or failure (Colvin and Ashman, 2010). The young people we spoke with did not fully appreciate the differentiation between the various people involved in supporting them. Rich, for example, referred to a member of the team who he regularly chats with. He was reminded that this person was in fact his support worker and not a peer mentor. Rich also did not realize that the contact he had with one of the peer mentors had been a form of peer mentoring, nor that he could be identified as a mentee. This is suggestive of limited clarity about the roles of the mentors within the scheme. NCHA staff acknowledged their infancy in supporting volunteer type activity within the organization:

> We are years behind in volunteering. For an organization as large as this, it's not good that we are years behind. It was so new and it was given to one person who does two other jobs as well. You've got some part-time volunteers who weren't invested into Wavelength. Maybe we were overambitious and not as honest as we should have been.
>
> (John, staff member)

As well as the complexity of staffing issues, the NCHA was mindful of the difficulties in matching mentors with mentees. A member of staff commented that 'some of the mentors we had, it was not appropriate for them to mentor each other in some cases. The pairing was problematic – we didn't come to a consensus of how we should do it or how it should work' (Precious, staff member).

In the light of this, it is not unexpected that the mentees we spoke with did not appear to differentiate between peer mentors and other personnel involved in supporting them. John had to be reminded by NCHA staff that some of the activities he had been involved in had been a component of the peer mentoring scheme. The same was true of Rich, who had not realized that a peer mentor had taken him to the gym and had provided advice and support in relation to using the equipment safely and also nutrition. Similarly,

Nicola had to be reminded by NCHA staff that she had experienced peer mentoring from four different peer mentors.

It was evident that peer mentoring covers a range of areas and is not solely focused on advice: it includes the development of skills, including cooking and, as stated above, gym work and nutrition. The lack of clarity in housing tenants' understanding of the role of a peer mentor could be associated with the varied activities put in place within the projects. There was limited differentiation between the activities, and the potential mentees tended to view any person as a potential source of support, particularly in their first few weeks of supported accommodation. NCHA staff acknowledged that there was a need for increased clarity about how the peer mentoring scheme should work and also about the delineation of roles across the variety of people involved with the projects. John said:

> Each individual has their own key worker and trying to get them involved with someone else – for some people it was 'Well, I have been to one, why would I go to someone else?' That goes back to how we promote it – it shouldn't be seen as a separate thing – it wasn't like peer mentoring.

Clarity of roles may not necessarily be an issue if the overall objective of the peer mentoring project is to build in additional levels of support for young people. However, in terms of tracking the success of interventions, some clarity about what peer mentors can provide would be helpful to mentees. NCHA staff identified the gap that the peer mentoring role attempted to bridge, so there was some clarity in what it was hoping to achieve:

> For those young people who see support, we don't do formal support, we like to keep it as informal as possible, but for those who see it as formal and who we can't support, that's the gap the [peer] mentor can fill. We need the mentor to support and vouch for us.
>
> (John, staff member)

The peer mentors valued their role in providing advice and guidance for the young people who required mentoring, and the advantages their age gave them (Checkoway and Gutiérrez, 2006). Poppy emphasized the advantages to the mentees of their involvement, and in doing so she also illuminated the personal journey that she had been on:

> Even if adults are trying to help, like older generations, it still feels like they're just saying, well in my day you didn't do that so just

like give your head a shake and just do it. So I think coming from us it seems more like, we're helping … they don't see us as telling them what to do … I think that's the good thing about all of us, we've all been in a situation where we've all been at that point where we've needed someone, so now we can be that someone.

(Poppy, peer mentor)

It was clear to the peer mentors what their roles were, even though this was less clear to the mentees. However, the mentors also described ad hoc interventions where they mentored informally. This tended to include, for example, family, friends and neighbours. While this type of mentoring goes beyond the remit of the Wavelength project, it is illustrative of the transferable skills mentors have gained from their involvement with the project. Being involved in mentoring supports young people in their move towards independence (Stein, 2006). Dianna emphasizes this:

I suppose you're a peer mentor wherever you go because wherever you go someone might ask you for advice, so then your role is quite wide, widely open … you can help anyone who you come across but it doesn't just mean that you have an official mentee, but you're always just helping someone, it's just how it works really.

(Dianna, peer mentor)

The mentors clearly understood their role and the boundaries around it. This is in part as a result of the systems in place to support mentors. Matching mentors and mentees is a key element of any peer mentoring programme (Hall and Jaugietis, 2011). While it is known for mentee–mentor relationships to develop informally (Noe, 1988), this was not appropriate for the young people in this study. The NCHA systematically matched mentors with mentees according to identified strengths, geographical location and age.

Supporting areas of need

It is not unusual for vulnerable young people to require support in areas that cause them difficulty (DuBois *et al.*, 2011). All of the young people who accessed mentors detailed large numbers of critical incidents which led them to seek support and advice. The type of information the young people required most frequently was centred on financial matters, accessing benefits being the most common. Out of the 39 mentor incidents recorded, 23 involved supporting residents with financial matters, including managing a budget, accessing benefits, organizing shopping so as to identify cheaper items, controlling spending and dealing with debt. Mentors were confident when dealing with financial queries: this could be a direct result of the success of the Sound as a Pound mentoring project which had preceded Wavelength. Rachel, who had participated in one of the mentor focus groups, felt that providing financial advice was a strength of hers, as she had experienced financial difficulties herself. She also highlighted the complexities faced by young people who find themselves in financial difficulties and their limited agency in being able to resolve the issues themselves. Rachel states:

> Some people need that extra help to go and seek the things they need. So it's ... people just sitting in their house and being in debt, but if they don't know how to access the services, then they're just going to get themselves into a bigger hole really, so they need someone there to try and push them in the right direction basically.

> (Rachel, peer mentor)

Rachel emphasizes the mentees' need for different forms of support in helping young people to deal with the issues they face. This was also mentioned by the mentees, who recognized the importance of accessing support from others, not necessarily peer mentors. Rich identified three key people in his life who he felt offered him the support he needed: his support worker, an old school teacher who he had lived with and his girlfriend's mother. Rich's responses tended to be slightly vague and lacking in detail. This could have been because of the research context (being interviewed by two strangers) or his limited trust in others (Henn *et al.*, 2007). He clearly had issues with anger and had spent some time involved with the youth justice system. His old school teacher was the 'go to' person, as Rich states:

> I'd probably ring Kimberley, she's like my mum ... she's my school teacher but obviously I moved in with her and that and then I was really naughty, so I got put on probation and kicked out ... she's like my mum, like any other mum would [help], that's it.

> (Rich, mentee)

Rich also alluded to a heavy reliance on others, mostly females, to help him. He talked of the females in his life in ways that were indicative of dependence: '[she] looks after me'; 'like she does my washing, she irons clothes, she well she don't really give me money but yeah, she looks after my money sometimes ...' Rich acknowledges that he would have problems if Kimberley, in particular, was not around to help and support him.

This level of dependency was not evident in the other two mentees interviewed, although they clearly required support in many areas. Nicola, for example, was attempting to obtain a job at the time of the study. NCHA staff were supporting her with applications and the process of attending interviews. Nicola, along with the other two mentees, did not have a clear idea of what she wanted to do. This is perhaps not unusual, as they all had a history of a problematic relationship with education. This limited aspiration or lack of a definitive career path featured in their narratives about their futures:

> I did want to work with children, that's where I was ... but I like the retail side of things as well so I'm not quite sure ... I did do that [a childcare course] but that's what I came out of [college] because I didn't get on with anyone and they was always arguing and I couldn't work with people that kept arguing with me for no reason.
>
> (Nicola, mentee)

> Ain't got a plan, just take it as it comes.
>
> (Rich, mentee)

> Well I've been thinking quite a lot of times what I want to do with my cooking skills, like get a job, go further, but there's like other jobs that I haven't experienced so it's like a mix match. So I have to figure out ... I have started doing catering but if not then do something different.
>
> (John, mentee)

Peer mentors knew the boundaries of their roles and the limitations of the advice they could provide (Colvin and Ashman, 2010). They were very clear that their role was not to provide solutions but to help the mentees arrive at their own. They used the words 'in a way you kind of negotiate them I'd say', 'steering in the right direction' and 'you're just telling them what they already know ... it's like you've planted it there but then they're just saying it' (Dianna, Rachel and Nicola, peer mentors). They also recognized that more needed to be done in relation to advertising the peer mentoring programme. Nicola states:

> We all kind of said it needed to be advertised a lot better, we needed to get the word out to the local community places, like the housing places a lot more so that they kind of knew where we was and they knew that we could help their tenants.

All peer mentors acknowledged that tenants experienced needs in a number of areas. They also explained how important it was for them to be able to give something to those who were experiencing issues similar to ones they had faced at the beginning of their own tenancies. Without exception, they agreed that the peer mentoring programme filled a gap in provision for young people who related more positively to people of their own age. This would suggest that peer mentoring has an important role to play in supporting homeless young people.

The potential for impact

From the limited number of surveys returned in which mentees had completed the parts that covered both pre- and post-involvement with the mentoring programme, the evidence would suggest that the programme had some impact. Table 11.1 illustrates the change that the young people identified for themselves.

Table 11.1 Wavelength entry and exit survey results: the identified impact of peer mentoring

A range of different career options are open to me	0	1	2	3	4	5	6	7	8	9	10
Entry					3		1				
Exit									1	1	2
I have the skills needed to do well in the workplace	0	1	2	3	4	5	6	7	8	9	10
Entry				2	1		1				
Exit									1	1	2
I like myself the way I am	0	1	2	3	4	5	6	7	8	9	10
Entry				1				1			2
Exit								1			3
I can bounce back after disappointment or when something goes wrong	0	1	2	3	4	5	6	7	8	9	10
Entry			1					1		1	1
Exit									1	1	2
I want to stay out of trouble	0	1	2	3	4	5	6	7	8	9	10
Entry											4
Exit											4

If I need help, I feel there are people there for me	0	1	2	3	4	5	6	7	8	9	10
Entry				1	1		2				
Exit										1	3
Overall, how satisfied are you with your life nowadays?	0	1	2	3	4	5	6	7	8	9	10
Entry					1	1		2			
Exit							1			1	2

It is evident from the pre-project surveys (see Table 11.2) that some young people face considerable challenges, particularly in relation to knowing that there is someone there for them. This information could pave the way for the provision of improved information to individuals about the availability of peer mentors.

Table 11.2 Pre-Wavelength involvement survey

A range of different career options are open to me	0	1	2	3	4	5	6	7	8	9	10
Entry		1		2	6	2	1	1	1		2
I have the skills needed to do well in the workplace	0	1	2	3	4	5	6	7	8	9	10
Entry					2	4	2	2	3		3
I like myself the way I am	0	1	2	3	4	5	6	7	8	9	10
Entry				1	1	1	1	3	2	2	5
I can bounce back after disappointment or when something goes wrong	0	1	2	3	4	5	6	7	8	9	10
Entry				1			1	3	2	4	5
I want to stay out of trouble	0	1	2	3	4	5	6	7	8	9	10
Entry											16
If I need help, I feel there are people there for me	0	1	2	3	4	5	6	7	8	9	10
Entry				1	1	2	1	1	4	2	4
Overall, how satisfied are you with your life nowadays?	0	1	2	3	4	5	6	7	8	9	10
Entry					2	3	3	2	2	2	2

The pre-Wavelength involvement surveys support the discussions we had with the three mentees. The latter described a lack of clarity about possible career options and about the difficulties they had experienced and continued to experience with education. Scores were skewed to the left of the scoring index, which is indicative of the low levels of self-esteem and resilience we also picked up during interviews. The three mentees all talked about depending on others but there being a lack of trust. This is perhaps not surprising given the trajectories they had been on: disruptive schooling experiences, being let down by family, involvement with youth justice systems. John emphasizes the difficulties he has with education as he explains why he doesn't attend:

> I did turn up for like the first year at college and then like the second year I've been like lagging behind. Most days I just don't go in because I get really stressed out because of what the staff will say or other students in different areas of the college …. If it's like maths, I'll be an hour late because I don't like maths or what other people think about me.
>
> (John, mentee)

He further indicates the difficulties that are involved with trust and the role that peer mentors can play in helping to rebuild trust in others:

> With me it takes time, sometimes it takes a couple of seconds to like talk to people … sometimes I talk to people and sometimes I don't because it's the way people react or how they sat to other people … the peer mentors came to this project, first like couple of days was like, let's just settle down and see what's going on. Sometimes I'm nervous to go and see them … but there's someone who can listen and I feel she's actually listening so that's one thing.

Being listened to is noted as important to young people who face a range of difficult situations (Holbeche, 1996). For John, it was really important that he felt listened to, and while he felt that college tutors did not take the time to really listen to what he had to say, this was not the case with the peer mentors, who John felt supported him primarily by listening. John recognized the impact that the housing project had had on his life, and although this is not directly linked to the peer mentoring scheme, the inclusion of peer mentoring is one of the ways in which the NCHA directly supports its young people.

Conclusion

The impact of being involved with the peer mentoring programme was more evident in those engaged with mentoring. This could be indicative of the stage of their individual journeys: the mentors had been involved with the NCHA for longer, had benefited from the support it provides and were further along in gaining their independence. In addition, they had all engaged positively with some form of education provision and as a result had some ideas of possible career paths. This was not the case for the mentees, who continued to have a sense of dependency on the resources of the NCHA and had limited thoughts about their futures: their main concerns were in the 'immediate' rather than what was to come. It is evident that the NCHA provides a vital role in supporting young people as they resolve their housing issues, but also as they determine how to get their lives back on track. The peer mentoring has a place in this, although there does need to be a more systematic introduction to tenants and tracking systems to ensure that impact can be measured effectively. While the programme is supported by volunteers and therefore has no ongoing cost implications, there are some costs involved with training the peer mentors effectively. At present, in-house training is provided by NCHA staff and this appears to have placed an additional burden on staff time during a period in which perhaps this was problematic because of staffing issues (such as high turnover rates and staff shortages).

In summary, the Wavelength programme resulted in some benefits for peer mentors, although the impact for mentees is not, at present, as evident. The young people living at the NCHA struggled to understand the different roles that support workers, mentors and other staff played in their lives. They could not differentiate the types of support that would be provided by the different groups, and this confusion had some influence on how the impact was perceived. However, as an additional layer of support, the peer mentoring programme supported the NCHA's ongoing interventions in supporting the development of self-confidence amongst its service users. Young people were appreciative of the types of activities the mentors led and talked positively about their input.

Chapter 12
Reflections and conclusions

This book has highlighted the plight of a number of young people who found themselves homeless. The main cause of their homelessness was a breakdown in family relations. There came a point in the individuals' lives where their connection with 'home' had become untenable. Their removal from the family home came about through either parental insistence that they leave or their own agency in wishing to remove themselves from a situation that was causing them immeasurable angst. Left behind in the wake of an abrupt end to their security was a vulnerable young person in need of shelter, support and intervention to repair the damage that had been caused to their self-esteem and confidence. This is in direct contradiction to what is usually associated with home, where

> [t]he trust which the child, in normal circumstances, vests in its caretakers, I want to argue, can be seen as a sort of *emotional inoculation* against existential anxieties – a protection against future threats and dangers which allows the individual to sustain hope and courage in the face of whatever debilitating circumstances she or he might later confront.
>
> (Giddens, 1991: 39; emphasis in original)

That emotional inoculation is manifested in the young people's apparent detachment from their current circumstances. As they recounted their histories, which frequently included tales of violence, aggression and a lack of family protection from such experiences, they did so with no apparent emotional connection. While this presentation may have been influenced by the research context itself, we were struck by the ways in which stories were told. The young people had clearly achieved sufficient distance from their experiences that they were able to recount them in an impartial way, possibly as part of the 'emotional and behavioural "formulae" which have come to be part of their everyday behaviour and thought' (ibid.: 44). Giddens goes on to state:

> Reconstruction of the past goes along with anticipation of the likely life trajectory of the future ... Holding a dialogue with time means identifying stressful events (actual events in the past and

possible ones to be faced in the future) and coming to terms with their implications.

(Giddens, 1991: 72, 73)

Such approaches to recounting their past experiences may have been an aspect of their coping strategies and a method for imagining a different future, but we did not delve into this area as part of this research project.

It was evident from the participants in this study that there is not one typical homeless young person. Some deployed high levels of agency in tackling their home situation and, following a 'final straw' argument, left their family home. This frequently resulted in them bedding down with friends and 'sofa surfing' until they were able to access the vital services needed to gain longer-term accommodation. Such individuals become hidden from the view of official statistics and it is evident from the data presented in Chapter 2 that the scale of the homelessness problem in the UK is difficult to fully appreciate. Snapshot counts provided by local authorities are therefore inadequate, both in measuring homelessness and as a means of allocating appropriate resources to tackle the problem. There needs to be a more reliable method through which accurate numbers of homeless people can be calculated. This would require additional resources for already stretched local authorities.

The Nottingham Community Housing Association fulfils the immediate need for shelter. In addition, the provision has an important role in bringing about lifestyle change for young people who have a complex history of disengagement from education and of drug taking in some cases and involvement in criminal activity in others. It is beyond doubt that the young people who accessed their services had a range of issues that required support and intervention. Many reported dysfunctional family backgrounds, which may have included parental violence, divorce and separation, or the introduction of step-parents which caused conflict and financial difficulties. In this context, the young people were left feeling isolated and socially neglected. Before becoming NCHA tenants, most had engaged with drugs, some had criminal records or continued to be involved with the police and all had struggled in education to a lesser or greater extent.

Many of the young people described being placed outside mainstream education. Their behavioural difficulties had resulted in their social isolation in education and their removal from 'normal' education. Bourdieu and Passeron (1977) refer to processes of elimination in education. They argue that young people who find themselves unaligned with the principles and processes of education either seek methods to secure their elimination or are eliminated on the basis of their poor behaviour. In both cases, the young people explained that they felt misunderstood by those who held positions of authority. It was evident from what the young people said that they had become a burden to education processes which had little time or resources to address the root of their problems. Sarah described spending whole days in the isolation unit, separated from her friends and not able to communicate with the other young people in the unit. In this situation, her limited belief in herself was further damaged as she struggled to contend with pressures of compliance in school, and also with some very serious family issues which had been, as she put it, 'swept under the carpet'.

It is evident that the troubled lives experienced by the young people in this study were linked to their inability to cope with the lack of intimacy and security within their home contexts. Stone *et al.* (2000: [2]) highlight the gradual decline of individuals as they face problematic situations:

> In considering the chain of events in these young people['s] lives it was clear that behaviours such as truancy and involvement in drug and alcohol abuse were symptoms of, and reactions to, a series of preceding events. Individuals did not usually set out to truant, neither did they suddenly decide to use drugs. More often, these behaviours were associated with a wider range of activities indulged in by the group of people of which they found themselves to be a part. However, underpinning these behaviours were a number of triggers each of which could be seen as providing the 'right' set of circumstances for problem behaviours to occur.

Similarly, the young people in this study also described 'falling into the wrong crowd' and being unduly influenced by the criminal activities of those around them, who tended to be older. Importantly, the young people did not seek out trouble. Their involvement with dubious activities was clearly the result of 'triggers', which, when combined, proved to be overly influential in the decisions they subsequently made. Some of the young people in the study recognized that their continued involvement in particular activities was holding them back from making changes. This was particularly the case for Darren, who knew he had to stop fighting in order to move forward. The lure of fighting continued to be an important aspect of his identity and he was currently unable to distance himself from it. The young people's decision making while at the NCHA was clouded by their apparent existence in an in-between life, one which was framed by a lived history and a projected future. Their capacity to make decisions about their futures was reduced by the immediacy of having to tackle the residual damage of their pasts.

There were many contradictions in the young people's narratives. While they longed for intimacy and closeness with others, this desire did not usually extend to other residents within the NCHA. There was a distinct lack of connectedness amongst housing association tenants, which could possibly be explained by the transient nature of the population. The young people predominantly stayed in their own rooms, only venturing out when they required support from their key worker or were involved in one of the planned community activities (e.g. cooking). This behaviour goes against what is considered to be our 'social inheritance', in which

> [a]nother characteristic which is perhaps important is our tendency to feel a common sense of identity and interdependence with those with whom we share food and resources as equals. They form the in-group, the 'us', with whom we empathize and share a sense of identity.
>
> (Wilkinson and Pickett, 2010: 209)

There was no sense in which the individuals in this study had formed any kind of community with other tenants. Although they shared communal spaces, they lived very much as individuals: there was no 'us' in the young people's narratives.

What was also lacking in their lives was the traditional supportive structures such as faith, youth groups, and an understanding of multiple societal constructs. This lack of comprehension determined that they could only occupy limited social strata, which contributed to their on-going difficulties.

As for the young people who decided to leave home, it was evident that they had not sought advice before making such a monumental decision. This was also the case for participants in Stone *et al.*'s study:

> Looking back, the participants often recognised that they were making decisions – leaving home, quitting school – at a very young age and without any advice or support. The decisions they made were rarely rational and often put them into a position where they had nothing at all – no home, no parents, no money, no security.
>
> (Stone *et al.*, 2000: 3)

From what our participants said, leaving home and removing themselves from contexts which significantly dented their confidence was a decision that came easily. While it is generally accepted that there will be an increase in conflict between parents and children as the latter move into adolescence

(Santrock, 2007), the level of conflict experienced by the young people in this study went beyond that which is usually easily resolved. Despite the position the decision to leave home had left them in – 'no home, no parents, no money, no security' – not one of the young people expressed regret at having left their family home. The young people were therefore in an appropriate space, in which support, guidance and intervention could be positively received.

Re-engaging young people with education was a key focus of the NCHA's work with the young people. Through this work, it became evident that the young people's histories of education, and the elimination that had caused them to have such poor experiences of school, took time to repair and rebuild. NCHA staff frequently became the conduit for communication between a young person and the new educational setting (usually a college). The importance of this work was emphasized by Darren, who relied heavily on his key worker's intervention to secure a re-entry into college.

A key focus of the NCHA's work with young people was to support their ongoing growth into independence. Indeed, '[b]ecoming an independent person has been viewed traditionally as one of the culminating achievements of child and adolescent development' (Wiley, Rose, Burger and Miller, 2004: 100). Important to the young people's journey to independence were the ways in which they were supported in developing increased confidence to make decisions on matters that directly affected them. This was achieved mainly through discussion with their key mentors but also as a result of living away from parents who had been overly interfering. Sarah was particularly keen to make her own decisions but knew she had first to compensate for failed exam results that had occurred as a result of her homeless status. Maslow's (1943) hierarchy of needs provides some explanation for the young people's ordering of activities as they address their contexts. The young people's basic needs were being met by the NCHA, and as a result they could begin to address other areas of their lives that required attention.

Despite the estrangement from the family home the young people had experienced, they continued to talk positively about reconciliation with family members. While they longed for a secure home environment, they appreciated that this might not occur with their immediate family but would be part of their future lives. The damage caused by dysfunctional family backgrounds is difficult to measure, but the legacy includes limited self-belief and confidence. For some young people who had been living at the NCHA for some time, the impact of the Association's work could be seen in the plans they were able to consider and make. Living independently and being responsible for a budget were viewed positively by all the young people in the study. Their newfound sense of self, in this context, illustrated competencies that they had not had to factor into day-to-day living while in the family home. Coping with difficult situations had led the young people in this study to become single-minded but also prematurely aged. At times, we had to remind ourselves that we were talking with young people aged 16.

Peer mentoring was a positive feature of the NCHA's services. Young people appreciated another person who could advise them on various elements of their lives that they struggled with. There is clearly some work to do before the peer mentoring provision realizes the ambitions that NCHA staff have for it. The foundations are in place for this to be a successful component of NCHA provision, but at present there are insufficient resources to move this programme forward in a way that would significantly influence the young people and bring about change in their lives. The young people in this study showed high levels of resilience and the capacity to self-reflect: they knew how they had ended up in their current positions and had some idea of how to move forward. They were, however, limited in the scope of what they were able to address without resorting to help and guidance from the NCHA. The peer mentoring programme has a role to play in facilitating increased levels of self-help amongst the NCHA population.

It is evident that homelessness is on the increase and that policy measures are insufficient to tackle this social issue. The young people had little understanding of the political landscape. This resulted in their neediness when accessing the support and help they required to improve their life chances: they occupied the Victorian construct of the 'undeserving poor' and were therefore expendable in terms of policy. Despite this, in accessing the support of the NCHA, they had taken the first steps in repairing their lives and carving out a future for themselves. Homelessness is a key concern and affects large numbers of individuals each year. Current policies do little to support vulnerable young people. If the needs of young people such as those in this study are to be seriously addressed, the exact scale of the problem needs to be understood. This can only be achieved through commitment to tackling what has become a serious social justice issue, an issue for which political discourse can lay the blame at the feet of the individuals affected.

Volunteer agreement for the role of peer mentor with the Wavelength Programme

This letter sets out what we can each reasonably expect from your peer mentoring role with Nottingham Community Housing Association. NCHA appreciates you volunteering with the Wavelength Programme and is committed to providing you with a supportive environment. We hope that you will find your volunteer experience enjoyable and rewarding.

1. Volunteer role

Your role as volunteer peer mentor is set out in the attached volunteer role description and starts on the date entered at the end of this document. We hope that you will usually be able to volunteer with us for a period of at least six months so that we can each get the most from the volunteering experience. However, we are flexible about when you volunteer, so please let us know if you would prefer a different arrangement.

We expect you to perform your voluntary role to the best of your ability and to follow our procedures and standards, including health and safety and equal opportunities. You can expect us to deal with you in accordance with our equal opportunities policy.

2. Background checks

NCHA supports vulnerable and disadvantaged people. We therefore have a responsibility to conduct background checks on anyone that works for us with the Disclosure and Barring Service. Until such time as we receive the report from the DBS, you are not authorised to conduct any activity relating to peer mentoring for this programme.

Should we become aware of a recorded serious offence, on receipt of the report from the Disclosure and Barring Service, Nottingham Community Housing Association reserves the right to end the Volunteer Agreement. If this occurs, you will be notified immediately.

3. Obligations

You are under no obligation to work for NCHA and it is not intended for you to be employed by us or make any payment of salary to you.

4. Induction and training

We will provide an induction explaining what we do and how volunteers fit within our organisation. We will provide training to assist you to meet the standards we expect from volunteers and information about the accredited qualifications you can access.

5. Supervision and support

Your main point of contact during your volunteering with us will be one of our Volunteer Co-ordinators. This person's name will be listed at the end of this document. You will have regular contact with your designated co-ordinator to agree targets and identify opportunities for your volunteering role and discuss any problems or complaints you may have.

6. Expenses

We will reimburse certain out-of-pocket expenses, such as transport costs, incurred in connection with your volunteering for us. Details of these expenses and how to claim them can be found in the expenses policy, which will be provided.

7. Illness

In order to help Wavelength to manage the programme, please inform your Volunteer Co-ordinator if you are unable to work due to sickness on any day on which you have arranged.

8. Insurance

We will provide adequate insurance cover for you while you are undertaking voluntary work that has been approved and authorised by your Volunteer Co-ordinator.

9. Time off

As you are not under any obligation to work for the organisation, you are entitled to take as much or as little time off as you choose, but please do give us sufficient notice, so that we have the opportunity to make alternative arrangements to cover for your absence.

10. Confidentiality

In the course of providing your volunteering services, you may have access to confidential information relating to the organisation or our clients. We expect you not to use or disclose this information to any person either during your volunteering experience with us or at any time afterwards. All records created (whether written or electronic) including accounts, documents and notes about the organisation and its activities and all copies and extracts of them made or acquired by you in the course of your work as a volunteer shall be:

- the organisation's property
- used for the organisation's purposes only
- returned to the organisation at any time on demand
- returned to the organisation without demand if you cease to be actively involved in the organisation's work.

11. Conduct

In addition to the above, you will be required to adhere to the following code of conduct:

- you must not exchange personal details such as telephone numbers, addresses (including home, and social media, etc.) between peer mentors and peer mentees
- you must have any mentoring activities that you have planned or arranged authorised by your Volunteer Co-ordinator – all telephone contact to arrange meetings or activities between mentors and mentees is to made through your Volunteer Co-ordinator
- you must conduct yourself in an appropriate manner whilst mentoring and refrain from using bad language, or making any prejudiced comments
- if any peer mentoring relationship develops into a personal relationship, you must inform your Volunteer Co-ordinator and end the mentoring relationship, immediately.

12. Leaving

We ask that you give us as much notice as possible if you want to stop volunteering with us, so that we can rearrange our rota, or find a suitable replacement. This arrangement is not intended to be a legally binding contract between us and may be cancelled at any time at the discretion of either party.

There is no intention to create an employment relationship with Nottingham Community Housing Association either now or at any time in the future. The only exception to this will be if we are able to identify a position that would be suitable for you to apply for.

Please acknowledge that you understand and agree to the contents of this letter by signing, dating and returning the enclosed copy. You must also keep a copy of this letter for reference.

Person	Name	Signature	Date
Volunteer Candidate			
Volunteer Co-ordinator			

Guidelines for peer mentor/ mentee interactions

Wavelength recognises that there will be occasions when volunteer peer mentors will be required to conduct one-to-one interactions with peer mentees. For volunteers to work alone with another person, all mentors must attend peer mentor training before being allowed to conduct interactions, and adhere to strict rules regarding meetings and activities.

Below is a list of guidelines that should be followed during a one-to-one meeting. This list is not exhaustive and certain precautions may be put in place relating to specific matches. A risk assessment, which will be conducted by the volunteer co-ordinator, will be carried out on each match/ event to highlight any additional steps that will need to be taken.

Guidelines for meeting peer mentees:

- A mentor should always put his or her own safety first.
- Meetings should *always* take place in a public place.
- Peer mentors should not arrange to meet at the mentee's home, unless they live in the same supported housing project, or unless agreed with the volunteer co-ordinator.
- End the meeting if you feel threatened or uncomfortable in any way.
- A mentor should never meet the mentee alone if they are unhappy with the prospect.
- A mentor should always ensure that the volunteer co-ordinator has authorised a meeting and is aware of the date, time and venue for any activity. The only exception to this would be if the peer mentor has reported an unplanned opportunity, where effective mentoring has taken place that can be counted as peer mentoring, to the volunteer co-ordinator. This should be the exception rather than the rule and authorised as a recorded activity at the discretion of the volunteer co-ordinator.
- At the beginning of a mentoring relationship, set clear and concise boundaries, agree to them and adhere to them at all times. Refer to them, if you feel you need to.

- End any meeting if the mentee is under the influence of alcohol or drugs and inform the volunteer co-ordinator immediately.
- If you have any concerns or worries about mentoring contact the volunteer co-ordinator as soon as possible.
- Never disclose any personal details to the person that you are mentoring, such as your address, phone number, Facebook/Twitter/ email address. Never agree to accept the mentee's details.
- In the event of an emergency, or if the peer mentor is unable to contact the volunteer co-ordinator, volunteers will be able to contact NCHA's out-of-hours team (SMaRT). This facility is to be used only in the event of an emergency.

Procedures for Wavelength staff and peer mentors/mentees

Procedure overview

This procedure sets out the process for Volunteer Co-ordinators to establish and maintain a one-to-one peer mentor/mentee relationship on the Wavelength Peer Mentoring Programme.

Procedure details

All candidates referring to the Wavelength programme (mentors or mentees) should go through the same process, in order for them to experience similar opportunities and management. For monitoring purposes (and data collection for the evaluation process) the candidates' demographic information, induction, training, activities and exit should be recorded on the Wavelength database. This information will be compiled for the programme evaluation, which will be conducted by Nottingham Trent University.

Recruitment
Referrals

Candidates for Wavelength may be introduced to the programme in one of three ways:

- recruited from a HWCS [Housing With Care and Support] Young Persons project (both ex and current service users)
- referred by an external organization
- self-referral

All candidates should complete a referral form or have an appropriate person complete the form on their behalf.

This document will provide the Volunteer Co-ordinator (or VC) with details of a referring organisation and contact persons, with whom they can liaise. It will also identify whether the candidate wishes to participate with the programme as:

- A peer **mentor** and specify the life skills areas in which they believe they can effectively support another young person, or
- A peer **mentee** and identify the areas where there is a skills deficit and what support the candidate requires.

For candidates that are recruited from HWCS projects, VCs can gather this information from project staff or the SuRe System. When a referral is received, the VC should record the relevant details of the young person on the appropriate database sections, for contact and monitoring.

The VC should arrange an appointment to interview the candidate and deliver an induction, by attempting to contact them using the following procedures:

- by phone on no more than three occasions, leaving voicemails if unanswered (and if the option to leave messages is available)
- by sending the candidate a text message on no more than three occasions
- by sending the candidate one letter, informing them that you need to meet with them and giving a time limit for responding.
- if no contact is made, liaise with the referring agency or project key worker, to ascertain whether they are still in contact with the candidate
- if no contact is made, record withdrawal of the candidate on the database.

Contacting candidates

Once contact has been established, the VC should make no more than three attempts to visit the candidate to deliver an induction interview. If phone contact is not maintained and visits are unsuccessful, the candidate should be withdrawn and notified by whichever means are available, i.e. phone, voicemail, email, letter, etc., and their withdrawal recorded on the database.

If the VC considers it appropriate, candidates can be deferred and remain on programme for an agreed period of time, not exceeding three months. This should be reviewed, prior to the deferral time coming to an end, to establish whether the candidate will return and participate with training and/or mentoring/being mentored.

Enrolment onto the programme

During the induction interview, the VC should assess the suitability of the candidate and ensure that all potential needs/risks have been identified and recorded. There are several forms to complete during the course of the interview; therefore, sufficient time is to be allocated in order to gather all relevant details. If further information is required, that a candidate is unable/unwilling to provide, the VC should obtain their permission to contact their referrer, in order to gather the appropriate details.

VCs are advised to complete the forms as quickly as possible, but if the candidate is reluctant to complete all of the documents at the induction interview, a second meeting can be arranged. However, the candidate should be made aware that the process will take longer if all the relevant information is not gathered in one meeting.

The VC is to conduct the following during an interview:

- A full description of the programme and expectations of candidates
- Completion of all appropriate paperwork (listed below)
- An explanation of why attendance at the peer mentoring training course is mandatory for all candidates
- An overview of the process for achieving a National Open College Network qualification in peer mentoring (Levels 1 & 2).

Application forms

All candidates for Wavelength must go through the application process, during which VC's will determine their suitability for participation on the programme. It will also provide the opportunity to identify if there is a life skills deficit in a mentor candidate that can be addressed with peer mentoring. Additionally, it will identify any basic or additional support needs required for candidates to participate thoroughly.

Candidates who wish to become a **peer mentor** should be assisted to complete an application form.

Candidates who wish to become a **peer mentee** should be assisted to complete an alternative form.

Disclosure and Barring

All peer mentors must be cleared through the Disclosure and Barring Service. The DBS process will be conducted by the VC, once candidates have agreed to take part and completed the application form and signed to give their permission for the DBS process to take place. Peer mentees do not need to complete this form. Peer mentor candidates will be required to provide identification as prescribed in the DBS guidance notes on the application form, before it can be submitted. All identification documents produced must be verified by the VC. A copy of each of the required documents must be signed by the VC and sent along with the DBS application to HR [Human Resources]. The process usually takes 2–4 weeks. DBS forms are available from the HR.

The report from the DBS will be delivered directly to the candidates' addresses. VCs must advise candidates that they will be required to produce the original document for examination and report any issues highlighted with line management and discuss to assess suitability for one-to-one interactions. Peer mentors will not be allowed to conduct one-to-one interactions with mentees until their suitability has been determined by the report and staff.

Volunteer agreement
On receipt of a satisfactory DBS report, the VC should ask the peer mentor to read and sign a volunteer agreement (a signed copy of the agreement is to be retained by the mentor for reference). The agreement will highlight what help, support and benefits the peer mentor can expect from Wavelength and NCHA. It will also describe the terms and conditions that the mentor will be required to adhere to.

Entry/exit survey
VCs are to conduct an Entry Survey in the interview for both mentors and mentees. This questionnaire gathers information about the candidate's current situation, which will go towards building statistics for the programme's commissioners. An interim survey (using the same form) should be conducted once the candidate has started their interactions, and once again on exit. If contact with the candidate is lost, the interim survey can be used as the exit survey.

Initial assessment
VCs are also to conduct a basic initial assessment to ascertain the candidates' ability to mentor other young people. This form will identify the educational abilities and aspirations and will provide additional information to determine the candidates' suitability for mentoring.

Consent forms
NCHA uses various media to promote and report on its programmes and their activities. Therefore, candidates should be advised that this practice requires their permission to take and use photos, record activities, write testimonials, etc., for programme and NCHA publications.

Induction record
VCs are advised to use an induction record to make sure that they have explained all of the details of the programme to the candidates. This will help to ensure that all elements of participation are explained and give the opportunity for the candidates to ask questions. Most elements of the

induction and the requirements of both the VC and the mentor will also be described on the Volunteer Agreement.

Post interview
Work Placement Details form

Once the paperwork process for each candidate has been completed (including receipt of a suitable report from the DBS) the VC should complete a Work Placement Details form and send it through to HR. This form details the position held within the organisation and the activities they will conduct, on behalf of the Wavelength programme.

Acceptance letter

Having sent the candidates' DBS forms to be processed by HR, candidates for peer mentoring should be informed officially of their acceptance onto the Wavelength programme by way of an acceptance letter. The letter specifies that they will only be permitted to conduct one-to-one interactions, once they are able to produce a report from the DBS with no events recorded that would preclude them from working with vulnerable young people. They can, however, begin the training process, in order to keep momentum going and to prepare them for working as a peer mentor.

Training

Candidates for peer mentoring should be made aware of the one-day training course, at the interview stage. This is a mandatory-attendance course, with no pass or fail element to it and students will receive an organisational certificate of attendance (not accredited).

Candidates will be required to attend this course, so that they are equipped with information to conduct activities appropriately, whilst operating on behalf of Wavelength and NCHA. It will also provide information of the programme and organisational protocols that peer mentors are to follow in the event of several different circumstances taking place, whilst conducting interactions.

Wavelength delivers its own in-house training and VCs should keep their line manager regularly updated with numbers of candidates, so that dates and venues can be arranged, in good time. Training courses are arranged regularly and in the local area of the candidates. For those living in outlying areas, transport will be made available. Once a candidate is at the stage of having completed training and been cleared through the DBS process, VCs can start to plan activities.

Planning interactions
Matching mentors with mentees
The Wavelength database of mentors and mentees together with specific areas of interest that they have identified as their particular strengths, in which they feel they can deliver effective support, will be updated regularly. This will enable VCs to select the appropriate mentor with which to match with the specific needs of a mentee. The areas of support are not exhaustive, but the main skills are listed on the application form.

Transport and activities expenses
When pairing a mentor with a mentee, particular attention should be given to where they live, to ensure that both are logistically able to maintain contact. The mentors' addresses will be recorded onto the database, so that the pairing can be set up in the same area.

If transport costs are incurred to attend meetings and one-to-one interactions, both the mentor and mentee can be refunded, providing they can both produce a valid public transport ticket on the specified date and local to the planned venue (including the return journey) in order to have travel costs fully reimbursed. Transport to interactions/activities by taxi is to be discouraged and allowed only in difficult circumstances and at the discretion of the VC.

The programme holds a limited budget for peer mentoring costs or purchasing of materials directly associated with one-to-one interactions. However, any activities requiring funds are to be agreed by the VC prior to them taking place, in order to establish the need and value-for-money aspect of the expense. As with refunding transport costs, a receipt is to be produced for any purchases, with only the expenses directly relating to the activity to be refunded. Staff should check receipts to ensure that they are valid and relate to agreed items and/or activities, before reimbursements are made.

Matching mentor/mentee
Once a mentor has been matched with a mentee, a meeting should be arranged at a neutral venue. The VC should be present to introduce the pair to each other and co-ordinate the meeting, to allow the VC to judge whether the pairing will be suitable and effective, in the beginning stages. All future communication between the mentor and the mentee to arrange activities should be made through staff.

If the pairing is successful, a further meeting should be arranged between all three parties, during which support planning should take place using SMART [Specific, Measurable, etc.] targets. (This can also be arranged at the point of the pair meeting, if both are happy to proceed with planning at that point.) However, FIWs should bear in mind that individuals may not immediately feel comfortable with their mentoring partner, so each should be given the time to speak with the VC in private in case they have any misgivings about the pairing.

If an initial meeting to pair a mentor with a mentee is unsuccessful (or found to be unsuitable at a later stage) the mentoring relationship should be ended. The VC should then look for alternatives. If no other options are presented, the VC will notify the mentor/mentee when a potential candidate becomes available.

Planning and recording activities/interactions

Once a constructive mentor/mentee relationship has been established and maintained, VCs should monitor activities and encourage participants to record the results of interactions and any positive progress made. Reviews should be conducted at regular and agreed intervals, during which targets can be acknowledged or amended. There are a variety of forms that can be used to record activities and interactions for both the mentor and the mentee. These are not prescribed, but participants should be encouraged to record as much detail as possible. This will enable the VC to observe the mentoring relationship and how effective it is.

All interactions and activities between mentors and mentees are to be recorded on the Wavelength database as soon as possible after the event.

Risk assessments

Generic risk assessments should be in place for all planned activities, whether supervised by or not, using the NCHA matrix for identifying levels of risk. This will help to maintain continuity and the effectiveness of interactions and will generate positive outcomes for data collection. Risk assessment training is available through the NCHA Training Department, via e-learning. All staff are to access this training, which can be set up through line management.

Interactions

Conduct of authorised interactions

Any interactions conducted between the mentor and mentee are to be agreed and authorised by the VC. They are to be planned in conjunction with the VC, the mentor and the mentee. Expenses are to be reimbursed after the activity and only on the production of valid receipts relating to the planned activity. The only exception to this will be if the VC knows of any costs involved prior to the event and if the VC can arrange payment. This will be at the discretion of the VC.

Missing planned interactions

Both parties are to be informed that if they are unable to attend a planned meeting/activity, they should contact the VC as soon as possible, in order for the VC to notify the other party and, if possible, to make alternative arrangements. Both parties should also be reminded that contact and arrangements should be made through the VC and not directly between the mentor and mentee. Both parties are to be encouraged to provide as much notice as possible, if they cannot attend an arranged meeting/activity.

Both parties are to be discouraged from missing planned appointments on a regular basis and informed that they would be putting their mentor/mentee position at risk, if this were to continue.

Both parties are to be instructed that if they turn up for a planned meeting and either the mentor or mentee does not attend, that they are to wait for no longer than 30 minutes, before they leave the venue planned for the activity. They should then report the missed appointment to the VC at the earliest opportunity.

Interactions conducted out of office hours

Interactions that are arranged and conducted out of the normal working hours of the VC are permitted, providing the VC has conducted the appropriate risk assessment and has appropriate control measures in place.

During normal office hours, both the mentor and the mentee will have the ability to contact their VC, or the Wavelength line manager. They will also be provided with out-of-hours emergency support provided by SMaRT. All candidates will be provided with the contact details for SMaRT by the VC and given the protocols with which to deal with a variety of situations, for situations specific to the activity, time and venue in which they should determine whether to access support. Participants will also be reminded of how to contact the emergency services.

Unauthorised interactions

Any activities conducted without the VC's knowledge are not to be recorded as an interaction on the Wavelength database. The mentors/mentees involved are to be referred to their volunteer agreement and referred to the policy regarding this event and reminded that, if similar situations occur, they are putting their position of being a volunteer at risk. The VC is to make a note of any unplanned interactions in the mentor/mentee's records.

The exception to the previous paragraph will only be accepted if the mentor reports an unplanned interaction between themselves and another person who is not enrolled as a mentee, but that they believe would make good evidence of an interaction, where they have delivered effective support in a controlled environment or public place. In this case, the VC is to determine the suitability of the interaction and, if appropriate to the programme, record it on the Wavelength database.

Monitoring the mentoring relationship

VCs should monitor mentoring relationships, to be aware if any pairing develops into an emotional/physical relationship and the potential safeguarding risks that may arise from this occurring. It should be stressed to both the mentor and the mentee at the induction stage (and reiterated if a relationship becomes apparent later on) that if this happens, the volunteering agreement has been breached and that the Wavelength mentoring relationship is to be ended immediately.

Mentors and mentees are to be discouraged from exchanging personal details such as telephone numbers, home/email addresses, or communicating through social media, etc.

However, it is accepted that VCs will have no control over pre-existing or newly found friendships that develop as a result of a mentoring relationship, particularly in HWCS.

VCs should also be vigilant to possible risks to both the mentor and mentee, should a friendship relationship deteriorate to the point whereby one or both parties would be affected in an adverse way.

If a relationship develops as described in the previous paragraphs, VCs should discuss issues with both parties to determine whether to continue or end the pairing. If it is agreed that it should, a risk assessment with suitable control measures is to be produced.

Enrolment onto the Open College Network programme

Mentors have the opportunity to obtain a recognised qualification in peer mentoring, whilst on programme. Registration, assessment, internal verification and certification fees will be covered by NCHA, therefore VCs should stress that there is an expectation that candidates will complete units.

Should a candidate express a desire to be enrolled onto the NOCN [National Open College Network] peer mentoring, the VC is to notify the line manager, who will arrange to meet the candidate and:

• Complete an induction and relevant forms to register with the training department

- Explain six months time limit for completion of units and extensions availability
- Offer one-to-one tutorials to support with evidence collection and portfolio building
- Assess completed units and forward on training department for internal verification
- Provide feedback and arrange certification.

Exiting the programme

All mentors/mentors that have participated positively are to be contacted on exiting the programme. If it is possible to set up a meeting, VCs should complete the exit survey in order to establish how effective the experience has been. Ideally, the candidate should complete the form they were provided with on entry, so they are able to measure the distance travelled on the programme. If a meeting is not possible, the VC should attempt to contact the mentor/mentee to complete the exit survey on their behalf.

All mentors that have participated positively are to be acknowledged with a letter of recognition from the VC. They are also to be offered a reference or summary relating specifically to their participation and highlighting the support they have provided.

For any candidates who leave the programme prematurely, or through having a mentoring relationship ended, the VC should send a letter detailing the dates and reason(s) for terminating the volunteering agreement and record it on the database.

References

Aaltonen, S. (2012) 'Subjective orientations to the schooling of young people on the margins of school'. *Young*, 20 (3): 219–35.

Adonis, A., and Pollard, S. (1998) *A Class Act: The myth of Britain's classless society*. London: Penguin.

Allan, G. (1985) *Family Life*. Oxford: Basil Blackwell.

— (1989) *Friendship: Developing a sociological perspective*. London: Harvester Wheatsheaf.

Allen, T.D., Russell, J.E.A. and Maetzke, S.B. (1997) 'Formal peer mentoring: Factors related to protégés' satisfaction and willingness to mentor others'. *Group and Organization Management*, 22 (4): 488–507.

Andreou, C. (2000) 'Adolescents in care: The sense of homelessness'. *Journal of Child Pyschotherapy*, 26 (1): 69–78.

Archer, L. (2003) 'Social class and higher education'. In Archer, L., Hutchings, M. and Ross, A. (eds) *Higher Education and Social Class: Issues of exclusion and inclusion*. London: RoutledgeFalmer, 5–20.

Arnold, C., Yeomans, J., Simpson, S. and Solomon, M. (2009) *Excluded from School: Complex discourses and psychological perspectives*. Stoke-on-Trent: Trentham Books.

Arthur, R. (2007) *Family Life and Youth Offending: Home is where the hurt is*. Abingdon: Routledge.

Aviles de Bradley, A.M. (2011) 'Unaccompanied homeless youth: Intersections of homelessness, school experiences and educational policy'. *Child and Youth Services*, 32 (2): 155–72.

Bachu, A. (2016) *Homelessness* (Lords In Focus LIF-2016-0046). London: House of Lords. Online. http://researchbriefings.parliament.uk/ResearchBriefing/Summary/LIF-2016-0046#fullreport (accessed 13 December 2016).

Balchin, P., and Rhoden, M. (2002) *Housing Policy: An introduction*. 4th ed. London: Routledge.

Barnes, J., Belsky, J., Broomfield, K.A., Melhuish, E. and the National Evaluation of Sure Start (NESS) Research Team (2006) 'Neighbourhood deprivation, school disorder and academic achievement in primary schools in deprived communities in England'. *International Journal of Behavioral Development*, 30 (2): 127–36.

Bauman, Z. (2001) *The Individualized Society*. Cambridge: Polity.

Behar, R. (1996) *The Vulnerable Observer: Anthropology that breaks your heart*. Boston: Beacon Press.

Bell, D.N.F., and Blanchflower, D.G. (2010) 'Young people and recession: A lost generation? (Dartmouth College Working Paper). Hanover, NH: Dartmouth College. Online. www.dartmouth.edu/~blnchflr/papers/Economic%20Policy%20Article%20v3_24.pdf (accessed 28 December 2016).

BERA (British Educational Research Association) (2011) *Ethical Guidelines for Educational Research*. London: BERA. Online. http://content.yudu.com/Library/A2xnp5/Bera/resources/index.htm?referrerUrl=http://free.yudu.com/item/details/2023387/Bera (accessed 2 February 2014).

Berridge, D., Beihal, N. and Henry, L. (2012) *Living in Children's Residential Homes* (Research Report DFE-RR201). London: DfE.

Billington, T., and Pomerantz, M. (2004) 'Resisting social exclusion'. In Billington, T., and Pomerantz, M. (eds) *Children at the Margins: Supporting children, supporting schools*. Stoke-on-Trent: Trentham Books, 1–13.

Bines, W. (1997) 'The health of single homeless people'. In Burrows, R., Pleace, N. and Quilgars, D. (eds) *Homelessness and Social Policy*. London: Routledge, 132–48.

Bochel, C. (2008) 'State welfare'. In Alcock, P., May, M. and Rowlingson, K. (eds) *The Student's Companion to Social Policy*. 3rd ed. Oxford: Blackwell Publishing, 189–95.

Bourdieu, P. (1990) *The Logic of Practice*. Trans. Nice, R. Cambridge: Polity Press.

— (1998) *Practical Reason*. Cambridge: Polity Press.

Bourdieu, P., and Passeron, J.-C. (1977) *Reproduction in Education, Society and Culture*. Trans. Nice, R. London: Sage.

Bowpitt, G. (1997) *Sleeping Rough in Nottingham*. Nottingham: Nottingham Help the Homeless Association.

Bramley, G., Fitzpatrick, S., Edwards, J., Ford, D., Johnsen, S., Sosenko, F. and Watkins, D. (2015) *Hard Edges: Mapping severe and multiple disadvantage: England*. London: Lankelly Chase Foundation.

Brooks, R. (2003) 'Young people's higher education choices: The role of family and friends'. *British Journal of Sociology of Education*, 24 (3): 283–97.

Brown, S. (2012) 'The latest statutory homelessness statistics for England'. Online. http://youthhomelessnortheast.org.uk/research-and-reports/the-latest-statutory-homelessness-statistics-for-england/ (accessed 4 March 2017).

Burgess, S., and Briggs, A. (2006) 'School assignment, school choice and social mobility' (CMPO Working Paper 06/157). Bristol: Centre for Market and Public Organisation. Online. www.bristol.ac.uk/media-library/sites/cmpo/migrated/documents/wp157.pdf (accessed 16 July 2016).

Burke, P. J. (2012) *The Right to Higher Education: Beyond widening participation*. London: Routledge.

Byrom, T. (2016) 'Education and social class: Examining the fuzziness of choice and belonging'. In O'Grady, A., and Cottle, V. (eds) *Exploring Education at Postgraduate Level: Policy, theory and practice*. Abingdon: Routledge, 88–97.

Byrom, T., and Lightfoot, N. (2013) 'Interrupted trajectories: The impact of academic failure on the social mobility of working-class students'. *British Journal of Sociology of Education*, 34 (5–6): 812–28.

Cameron, H., McKaig, W. and Taylor, S. (2003) *Crossing the Threshold: Successful learning provision for homeless people*. London: Learning and Skills Development Agency.

Cassidy, T., and Lynn, R. (1991) 'Achievement motivation, educational attainment, cycles of disadvantage and social competence: Some longitudinal data'. *British Journal of Educational Psychology*, 61 (1): 1–12.

Centre for Social Justice (2013) *Fractured Families: Why stability matters*. London: Centre for Social Justice.

Centrepoint (2016) 'Youth homelessness: The issue'. Online. https://centrepoint.org.uk/youth-homelessness/the-issue/ (accessed 15 December 2016).

Checkoway, B.N., and Gutiérrez, L.M. (2006) 'Youth participation and community change: An introduction'. *Journal of Community Practice*, 14 (1–2): 1–9.

Clapham, D., Mackie, P., Orford, S., Thomas, I. and Buckley, K. (2014) 'The housing pathways of young people in the UK'. *Environment and Planning A*, 46 (8): 2016–31.

Clarke, A., Burgess, G., Morris, S. and Udagawa, C. (2015) *Estimating the Scale of Youth Homelessness in the UK: Final report*. Cambridge: Cambridge Centre for Housing and Planning Research.

CMHC (Canada Mortgage and Housing Corporation) (2004) 'Transitional housing: Objectives, indicators of success and outcomes' (Research Highlight: Socio-economic Series 04-017). Ottawa: CMHC. Online. www.cmhc-schl.gc.ca/odpub/pdf/63445.pdf?fr=1436636305301 (accessed 11 July 2015).

Colvin, J.W., and Ashman, M. (2010) 'Roles, risks, and benefits of peer mentoring relationships in higher education'. *Mentoring and Tutoring: Partnership in Learning*, 18 (2): 121–34.

Cook-Sather, A. (2006) 'Sound, presence, and power: "Student voice" in educational research and reform'. *Curriculum Inquiry*, 36 (4): 359–90.

Couch, J., Durant, B. and Hill, J. (2014) 'Uncovering marginalised knowledges: Undertaking research with hard-to-reach young people'. *International Journal of Multiple Research Approaches*, 8 (1): 15–23.

Crisis (n.d.) 'Critical condition: Homeless people's access to GPs' (media brief). Crisis UK. Online. www.crisis.org.uk/data/files/document_library/policy_reports/gp_mediabrief.pdf (accessed 9 March 2017).

— (2006) Homeless people and learning & skills: participation, barriers and progression. London: Crisis. Online. www.studylib.net/doc/8759359/homeless-people-and-learning-and-skills

— (2012) 'Young, hidden and homeless' (Research briefing). London: Crisis. Online. www.crisis.org.uk/data/files/publications/Crisis%20briefing%20-%20youth%20homelessness.pdf (accessed 14 December 2016).

— (2014) 'Work and skills'. Online. www.crisis.org.uk/pages/work-and-skills.html (accessed 9 March 2017).

— (2016a) 'About homelessness' (Briefing). London: Crisis. Online. www.crisis.org.uk/data/files/publications/Homelessness%20briefing%202016%20EXTERNAL.pdf (accessed 14 December 2016).

— (2016b) *The Homeless Monitor: England 2016* London: Crisis. Online. www.crisis.org.uk/data/files/publications/Homelessness_Monitor_England_2016_FINAL_(V12).pdf (accessed 1 April 2017).

Cullen, S. (2004) *Mediation for Young Homeless People: A good practice guide*. London: Shelter.

Dalton, M.M. and Pakenham, K.I. (2002) 'Adjustment of homeless adolescents to a crisis shelter: Application of a stress and coping model'. *Journal of Youth and Adolescence*, 31 (1): 79–89.

DCLG (Department for Communities and Local Government) (2010) *Evaluating the Extent of Rough Sleeping: A new approach*. London: DCLG. Online. www.gov.uk/government/uploads/system/uploads/attachment_data/file/6009/1713784.pdf (accessed 28 December 2016).

— (2012a) *Making Every Contact Count: A joint approach to preventing homelessness*. London: DCLG. Online. www.gov.uk/government/uploads/system/uploads/attachment_data/file/7597/2200459.pdf (accessed 4 March 2017).

— (2012b) *The Troubled Families Programme: Financial framework for the Troubled Families programme's payment-by-results scheme for local authorities*. London: DCLG. Online. www.gov.uk/government/uploads/system/uploads/attachment_data/file/11469/2117840.pdf (accessed 4 March 2017).

— (2015a) 'English indices of deprivation 2015'. London: DCLG. Online. www.gov.uk/government/statistics/english-indices-of-deprivation-2015 (accessed 15 December 2016).

— (2015b) *Statutory Homelessness: July to September Quarter 2015 England*. London: DCLG. Online. www.gov.uk/government/uploads/system/uploads/attachment_data/file/486671/2015_Q3_Statutory_Homelessness.pdf (accessed 18 March 2017).

— (2016a) 'Live tables on homelessness'. Online. www.gov.uk/government/statistical-data-sets/live-tables-on-homelessness (accessed 14 December 2016).

— (2016b) *Rough Sleeping Statistics Autumn 2015, England*. London: DCLG. Online. www.gov.uk/government/uploads/system/uploads/attachment_data/file/503015/Rough_Sleeping_Autumn_2015_statistical_release.pdf (accessed 28 December 2016).

— (2016c) *Statutory Homelessness, January to March 2016, and Homelessness Prevention and Relief 2015/16: England* (Housing: Statistical Release). London: DCLG. Online. www.gov.uk/government/uploads/system/uploads/attachment_data/file/533099/Statutory_Homelessness_and_Prevention_and_Relief_Statistical_Release_January_to_March_2016.pdf (accessed 28 December 2016).

DCSF (Department for Children, Schools and Families) (2008) *Reducing the Number of Young People Not in Education, Employment or Training (NEET): The strategy*. Nottingham: DCSF.

—'Provision of accommodation for 16 and 17 year old young people who may be homeless and/or require accommodation'. London: DCSF. Online. www.gov.uk/government/uploads/system/uploads/attachment_data/file/8260/Provision_20of_20accommodation.pdf (accessed 12 April 2015).

Delsing, M.J.M.H., Van Aken, M.A.G., Oud, J.H.L., De Bruyn, E.E.J. and Scholte, R.H.J. (2005) 'Family loyalty and adolescent problem behavior: The validity of the family group effect'. *Journal of Research on Adolescence*, 15 (2): 127–50.

Deuchar, R. (2009) *Gangs, Marginalised Youth and Social Capital*. Stoke-on-Trent: Trentham Books.

DfE (Department for Education) (2014) 'Promoting fundamental British values as part of SMSC in schools: Departmental advice for maintained schools'. London: DfE. Online. www.gov.uk/government/uploads/system/uploads/attachment_data/file/380595/SMSC_Guidance_Maintained_Schools.pdf (accessed 4 March 2017).

— (2016) 'Social mobility package unveiled by Education Secretary'. Press Release. Online. www.gov.uk/government/news/social-mobility-package-unveiled-by-education-secretary (accessed 28 December 2016).

DfES (Department for Education and Skills) (2003) *Widening Participation in Higher Education*. London: DfES.

Diaz, R. (2006) 'Street homelessness' (Factsheet). London: Shelter.

Doherty, J., and Hughes, M. (2009) *Child Development: Theory and practice 0–11*. Harlow: Pearson Education.

DuBois, D.L., Portillo, N., Rhodes, J.E., Silverthorn, N. and Valentine, J.C. (2011) 'How effective are mentoring programs for youth? A systematic assessment of the evidence'. *Psychological Science in the Public Interest*, 12 (2): 57–91.

Featherstone, B. (2004) *Family Life and Family Support: A feminist analysis*. Basingstoke: Palgrave Macmillan.

Ferguson, K.M., Kim, M.A. and McCoy, S. (2011) 'Enhancing empowerment and leadership among homeless youth in agency and community settings: A grounded theory approach'. *Child and Adolescent Social Work Journal*, 28 (1): 1–22.

Fielding, M. (2004) 'Transformative approaches to student voice: Theoretical underpinnings, recalcitrant realities'. *British Educational Research Journal*, 30 (2): 295–311.

Fitzpatrick, S. (2005) 'Explaining homelessness: A critical realist perspective'. *Housing, Theory and Society*, 22 (1): 1–17.

Fitzpatrick, S., Pawson, H., Bramley, G. and Wilcox, S. (2012) *The Homelessness Monitor: England 2012*. London: Crisis.

Fitzpatrick, S., Pawson, H., Bramley, G., Wilcox, S. and Watts, B. (2015) *The Homelessness Monitor: England 2015*. London: Crisis.

— (2016) *The Homelessness Monitor: England 2016*. London: Crisis.

Franks, M., Hunwicks, R., and Goswami, H. (2015) 'Barriers to the uptake of emergency accommodation by young runaways and thrown-out children and the role of the "transitional person"'. *Children and Society*, 29 (2): 146–56.

Fraser, N. (1997) *Justice interruptus: Critical reflections on the 'postsocialist' condition*. New York: Routledge.

— (2003) 'Social justice in the age of identity politics: Redistribution, recognition and participation'. In Fraser, N. and Honneth, A. *Redistribution or Recognition? A political-philosophical exchange*. London and New York: Verso.

— (2005) 'Reframing justice in a globalizing world'. *New Left Review*, 36, 69–88.

Fubra (n.d.) ourproperty.co.uk/guides/housing_association-p1.html (accessed 25 March 2017).

Gaetz, S., and Scott, F. (2012) *Live, Learn, Grow: Supporting transitions to adulthood for homeless youth*. Toronto: Canadian Homelessness Research Network Press. Online. http://homelesshub.ca/sites/default/files/foyer_report23112012.pdf (accessed 4 March 2017).

Gallarin, M., and Alonso-Arbiol, I. (2012) 'Parenting practices, parental attachment and aggressiveness in adolescence: A predictive model'. *Journal of Adolescence*, 35 (6): 1601–10.

Gauldie, E. (1974) *Cruel Habitations: A history of working-class housing, 1780–1918*. London: Allen and Unwin.

Gelles, R.J. (1997) *Intimate Violence in Families*. 3rd ed. Thousand Oaks, CA: Sage.

Giddens, A. (1991) *Modernity and Self-Identity: Self and society in the late modern age*. Cambridge: Polity Press.

Gilligan, R. (1999) 'Enhancing the resilience of children and young people in public care by mentoring their talents and interests'. *Child and Family Social Work*, 4 (3): 187–96.

Gingerbread (2017) 'Statistics: Single parents today'. Online. https://gingerbread.org.uk/content/365/Statistics (accessed 26 March 2017).

Glaser, N., Hall, R., and Halperin, S. (2006) 'Students supporting students: The effects of peer mentoring on the experiences of first year university students'. *Journal of the Australia and New Zealand Student Services Association*, 27: 4–17.

GOV.UK (2016) 'Check school performance tables'. Online. www.gov.uk/school-performance-tables (accessed 18 December 2016).

— (2017) 'Current registered providers of social housing: List of registered providers at 3 April 2017'. Homes and Communities Agency. Online. www.gov.uk/government/publications/current-registered-providers-of-social-housing (accessed 6 April 2017).

Greene, M.T. and Puetzer, M. (2002) 'The value of mentoring: A strategic approach to retention and recruitment'. *Journal of Nursing Care Quality*, 17 (1): 63–70.

Greve, J. (1997) 'Preface: Homelessness then and now'. In Burrows, R., Pleace, N. and Quilgars, D. (eds) *Homelessness and Social Policy*. London: Routledge, xi–xvii.

Gwadz, M.V., Gostnell, K., Smolenski, C., Willis, B., Nish, D., Nolan, T.C., Tharaken, M. and Ritchie, A.S. (2009) 'The initiation of homeless youth into the street economy'. *Journal of Adolescence*, 32 (2): 357–77.

Hall, R., and Jaugietis, Z. (2011) 'Developing peer mentoring through evaluation'. *Innovative Higher Education*, 36 (1): 41–52.

Harris, B. (2011) *Working with Distressed Young People*. Exeter: Learning Matters.

Hawthorne, J., Jessop, J., Pryor, J., and Richards, M. (2003) *Supporting Children through Family Change: A review of interventions and services for children of divorcing and separating parents*. York: Joseph Rowntree Foundation.

Hayatbakhsh, R., Clavarino, A.M., Williams, G.M., Bor, W., O'Callaghan, M.J., and Najman, J.M. (2013) 'Family structure, marital discord and offspring's psychopathology in early adulthood: A prospective study'. *European Child and Adolescent Psychiatry*, 22 (11): 693–700.

Henn, M., Weinstein, M., and Hodgkinson, S. (2007) 'Social capital and political participation: Understanding the dynamics of young people's political disengagement in contemporary Britain'. *Social Policy and Society*, 6 (4): 467–79.

Hodkinson, P. (2008) 'Understanding career decision-making and progression: Careership revisited'. John Killeen Memorial Lecture, Woburn House, London, 16 October 2008. Online. www.crac.org.uk/cms/files/upload/fifth_johnkilleenlecturenotes.pdf (accessed 29 December 2016).

Holbeche, L. (1996) 'Peer mentoring: The challenges and opportunities'. *Career Development International*, 1 (7): 24–7.

Holmes, J., and Kiernan, K. (2010) 'Fragile families in the UK: Evidence from the Millennium Cohort Study'. Draft report, June. Online. www.york.ac.uk/media/spsw/documents/research-and-publications/HolmesKiernan2010FragileFamiliesInTheUKMillenniumCohort.pdf (accessed 29 March 2017).

Holtrop, K., McNeil, S., and McWey, L.M. (2015) '"It's a struggle but I can do it. I'm doing it for me and my kids": The psychosocial characteristics and life experiences of at-risk homeless parents in transitional housing'. *Journal of Marital and Family Therapy*, 41 (2): 177–91.

Homeless Link (2014a) 'The unhealthy state of homelessness: Health audit results 2014'. Online. www.homeless.org.uk/sites/default/files/site-attachments/The%20unhealthy%20state%20of%20homelessness%20FINAL.pdf (accessed 9 March 2017).

— (2014b) 'Young and homeless 2013'. London: Homeless Link. Online. www.homeless.org.uk/sites/default/files/site-attachments/Youth%20and%20Homeless%202013%20Full%20Report.pdf (accessed 4 March 2017).

— (2014c) 'Young and homeless 2014'. London: Homeless Link. Online. www.homeless.org.uk/sites/default/files/site-attachments/201411%20-%20Young%20and%20Homeless%20-%20Full%20Report.pdf (accessed 4 March 2017).

— (2015) 'Young and homeless 2015'. London: Homeless Link. Online. www.homeless.org.uk/sites/default/files/site-attachments/201512%20-%20Young%20and%20Homeless%20-%20Full%20Report.pdf (accessed 15 December 2016). (The copyright date of 2014 in the publication is clearly erroneous.)

Hugman, R., Pittaway, E. and Bartolomei, L. (2011) 'When "do no harm" is not enough: The ethics of research with refugees and other vulnerable groups'. *British Journal of Social Work*, 41 (7): 1271–87.

Jagger, G., and Wright, C. (eds) (1999) *Changing Family Values*. London: Routledge.

Johnsen, S., Cloke, P. and May, J. (2005). 'Day centres for homeless people: Spaces of care or fear?' *Social & Cultural Geography*, 6 (6), 787–811.

Johnsen, S., Watts, B. and Fitzpatrick, S. (2016) 'First wave findings: Homelessness'. York: Welfare Conditionality. Online. www.welfareconditionality.ac.uk/wp-content/uploads/2016/05/WelCond-findings-homelessness-May16.pdf (accessed 19 March 2017).

Jones, G. (1995) 'Leaving home' (CES Briefing 2). Centre for Educational Sociology, University of Edinburgh. Online. www.ces.ed.ac.uk/briefings/ (accessed 12 April 2015).

Joseph Rowntree Foundation (1995) 'Foyers for young people' (Findings 142 (Housing Research), April).

Karcher, M.J., Kuperminc, G.P., Portwood, S.G., Sipe, C.L. and Taylor, A.S. (2006) 'Mentoring programs: A framework to inform program development, research, and evaluation'. *Journal of Community Psychology*, 34 (6): 709–25.

Kemp, P., Bradshaw, J., Dornan, P., Finch, N. and Mayhew, E. (2004) 'Routes out of poverty: A review of existing research evidence on what can help people out of poverty'. York: Joseph Rowntree Foundation. Online. www.jrf.org.uk/report/routes-out-poverty (accessed 3 April 2017).

Kennedy, C., and Fitzpatrick, S. (2001) 'Begging, rough sleeping and social exclusion: Implications for social policy'. *Urban Studies*, 38 (11): 2001–16.

Keogh, A.F., Halfpenny, A.M. and Gilligan, R. (2006) 'Children and young people in families living in emergency accommodation: An Irish perspective'. *Children and Society*, 20 (5): 360–75.

Kraus, D., Woodward, J. and Greenberg, T. (Eberle Planning and Research) (2007) *Vancouver Youth Housing Options Study*. Vancouver: Vancouver Youth Funders Table.

Kuhn, A. (2002) *Family Secrets: Acts of memory and imagination*. New ed. London: Verso.

Larson, A.M., and Meehan, D.M. (2011) 'Homeless and highly mobile students: A population-level description of the status of homeless students from three school districts'. *Journal of Children and Poverty*, 17 (2): 187–205.

Leibig, A.L., and Green, K. (1999) 'The development of family loyalty and relational ethics in children'. *Contemporary Family Therapy*, 21 (1): 89–112.

legislation.gov.uk (2017) 'Vagrancy Act 1824'. Online. www.legislation.gov.uk/ukpga/Geo4/5/83/section/4 (accessed 19 March 2017).

Lowe, R. (2005) *The Welfare State in Britain Since 1945*. 3rd ed. Basingstoke: Palgrave Macmillan.

MacInnes, T., Tinson, A., Hughes, C., Born, T.B., and Aldridge, H. (2015) *Monitoring Poverty and Social Exclusion 2015*. York: Joseph Rowntree Foundation.

Malpass, P. (2000a) *Housing Associations and Housing Policy: A historical perspective*. Basingstoke: Macmillan.

— (2000b) 'The discontinuous history of housing associations in England'. *Housing Studies*, 15 (2): 195–212.

Maslow, A. (1943) 'A theory of human motivation'. *Psychological Review*, 50, 370–96.

Masten, A.S. (2011) 'Resilience in children threatened by extreme adversity: Frameworks for research, practice, and translational synergy'. *Development and Psychopathology*, 23 (2): 493–506.

McNaughton, C. (2008) *Transitions through Homelessness: Lives on the edge*. Basingstoke: Palgrave Macmillan.

Mirza, H.S. (2009) *Race, Gender and Educational Desire: Why black women succeed and fail*. London: Routledge.

Mooney, A., Oliver, C. and Smith, M. (2009) *Impact of Family Breakdown on Children's Well-Being: Evidence review* (Research Report DCSF-RR113). London: DCSF.

Mooney, C.G. (2010) *Theories of Attachment: An introduction to Bowlby, Ainsworth, Gerber, Brazelton, Kennell and Klaus*. St Paul, MN: Redleaf Press.

Morphy, L. (2012) 'Foreword'. In Fitzpatrick, S., Pawson, H., Bramley, G. and Wilcox, S. *The Homelessness Monitor: England 2012*. London: Crisis, vii.

Mullender, A., Hague, G., Imam, U., Kelly, L., Malos, E. and Regan, L. (2002) *Children's Perspectives on Domestic Violence*. London: Sage.

Mullins, D. and Murie, A. (2008) 'Housing'. In P. Alcock, M. Way and K. Rowlinson (eds) *The Student's Companion to Social Policy, Third Edition*. Oxford: Blackwell Publishing (352–358).

Mullins, D. (2000) 'Social origins and transformations: The changing role of English housing associations'. *Voluntas: International Journal of Voluntary and Nonprofit Organizations*, 11 (3): 255–75.

Murie, A. (2008) 'Housing'. In Alcock, P., May, M. and Rowlingson, K. (eds) *The Student's Companion to Social Policy*. 3rd ed. Oxford: Blackwell Publishing, 343–50.

Neale, J. (1997) 'Homelessness and theory reconsidered'. *Housing Studies*, 12 (1): 47–61.

Nebbitt, V.E., House, L.E., Thompson, S.J., and Pollio, D.E. (2007) 'Successful transitions of runaway/homeless youth from shelter care'. *Journal of Child and Family Studies*, 16 (4): 545–55.

Newman, T., and Blackburn, S. (2002) 'Transitions in the lives of children and young people: Resilience factors'. *Interchange*, 78. Online. www.gov.scot/Resource/Doc/46997/0024005.pdf (accessed 11 December 2016).

Noe, R.A. (1988) 'An investigation of the determinants of successful assigned mentoring relationships'. *Personnel Psychology*, 41 (3): 457–79.

Noltemeyer, A., Bush, K., Patton, J. and Bergen, D. (2012) 'The relationship among deficiency needs and growth needs: An empirical investigation of Maslow's theory'. *Children and Youth Services Review*, 34 (9): 1862–7.

Nottingham City Council (2014) 'Homelessness Prevention Strategy data review – year one'. Online. https://nottinghaminsight.org.uk/f/64986/Library/Housing/Key-Strategies-and-Plans/ (accessed 15 December 2016).

— (2015) 'Multi agency process guidance: Supporting young people aged 16 or 17 years old who are at risk of homelessness'. Nottingham: Nottingham City Council. Online. https://nottinghaminsight.org.uk/f/64986/Library/Housing/Key-Strategies-and-Plans/ (accessed 15 December 2016).

Nottingham Workplace Chaplaincy (2012) 'Poverty and homelessness action: An introduction to faith-led community projects'. Online. www.nottinghamworkplacechaplaincy.org.uk/PDF_files/FaithAction%20Nottingham%20directory%20of%20projects.pdf (accessed 15 December 2016).

Nottinghamshire Homeless Watch (2015) 'Nottinghamshire Homeless Watch 2015: Headline findings'. Nottingham: Hostels Liaison Group. Online. www.rushcliffe.gov.uk/media/rushcliffe/media/documents/pdf/housing/HLG_finalHWreport2015.pdf (accessed 16 December 2016).

OECD (2011) 'Society: Governments must tackle record gap between rich and poor, says OECD'. Online. www.oecd.org/newsroom/societygovernmentsmusttacklerecordgapbetweenrichandpoorsaysoecd.htm (accessed 6 April 2017).

Office of National Statistics (2014) 'Families by family type'. Census 2011 data. Online. familiesbyfamilytype2001and2011_tcm77-360615.xls from http://webarchive.nationalarchives.gov.uk (accessed 27 March 2017).

Opinion Leader Research (2006) 'Homeless people and learning & skills: Participation, barriers and progression'. London: Crisis UK. Online. www.crisis.org.uk/data/files/document_library/research/homeless_people_and_learning_and_skills.pdf (accessed 9 March 2017).

Orb, A., Eisenhauer, L. and Wynaden, D. (2000) 'Ethics in qualitative research'. *Journal of Nursing Scholarship*, 33 (1): 93–6.

Overall, C. (1995) 'Nowhere at home: Toward a phenomenology of working-class consciousness'. In Barney Dews, C.L. and Leste Law, C. (eds) *This Fine Place So Far from Home: Voices of academics from the working class*. Philadelphia, PA: Temple University Press, 209–20.

Owen, J. (2015) 'Youth homelessness figure eight times higher than Government admits, says charity'. *The Independent*, 10 October.

Pahl, R.E. (2000) *On Friendship*. Cambridge: Polity.

Peart, S. (2013) *Making Education Work: How Black men and boys navigate the further education sector*. London: Trentham Books/Institute of Education Press.

Peart, S., and Atkins, L. (2011) *Teaching 14–19 Learners in the Lifelong Learning Sector*. Exeter: Learning Matters.

Pittaway, E., Bartolomei, L. and Hugman, R. (2010) '"Stop stealing our stories": The ethics of research with vulnerable groups'. *Journal of Human Rights Practice*, 2 (2): 229–51.

Platt, L. (2011) *Understanding Inequalities: Stratification and difference.* Cambridge: Polity.

Pleace, N. (1997) 'Rehousing single homeless people'. In Burrows, R., Pleace, N. and Quilgars, D. (eds) *Homelessness and Social Policy*. London: Routledge, 159–71.

— (2000) 'The new consensus, the old consensus and the provision of services for people sleeping rough'. *Housing Studies*, 15 (4): 581–94.

Powney, J. (2001) 'Homeless and a student at school'. *Journal of In-Service Education*, 27 (3): 361–76.

Public Health England (2014) 'Child health profile: March 2014: Nottingham'. Nottingham: Public Health England. Online. www.chimat.org.uk/resource/view. aspx?RID=192012 (accessed 15 December 2016).

Quilgars, D., and Anderson, I. (1997) 'Addressing the problem of youth homelessness and unemployment: The contribution of foyers'. In Burrows, R., Pleace, N., and Quilgars, D. (eds) *Homelessness and Social Policy*. London: Routledge, 216–28.

Quilgars, D., Johnsen, S., and Pleace, N. (2008) *Youth Homelessness in the UK: A decade of progress?* York: Joseph Rowntree Foundation.

Quilgars, D., and Pleace, N. (1999) 'Housing and support services for young people'. In Rugg, J. (ed.) *Young People, Housing and Social Policy*. London: Routledge, 109–26.

Ravenhill, M. (2008) *The Culture of Homelessness*. Aldershot: Ashgate.

Reay, D. (2001) 'Finding or losing yourself? Working-class relationships to education'. *Journal of Education Policy*, 16 (4): 333–46.

Reay, D., David, M.E., and Ball, S. (2005) *Degrees of Choice: Social class, race and gender in higher education*. Stoke-on-Trent: Trentham Books.

Riddell, R. (2010) *Aspiration, Identity and Self-Belief: Snapshots of social structure at work*. Stoke-on-Trent: Trentham Books.

Robertson, D.F. (2006) 'Homeless students: A search for understanding'. *International Journal of Leadership in Education*, 1 (2), 155–68.

Rogers, C.R., Dorfman, E., Gordon, T. and Hobbs, N. (2003) *Client-Centered Therapy: Its current practice, implications and theory*. New ed. London: Constable.

Rohde, L.A. (2013) 'The relevance of family variables in child and adolescent mental health'. *European Child and Adolescent Psychiatry*, 22 (11): 651–2.

Runkle, G. (1958) 'Some considerations on family loyalty'. *Ethics*, 68 (2): 131–6.

Santrock, J.W. (2007) *Child Development*. 11th ed. New York: McGraw-Hill.

Shelter (2014) 'Legal definition of homelessness'. Online. http://england.shelter.org. uk/get_advice/homelessness/homelessness_-_an_introduction/legal_definition_ of_homelessness (accessed 14 December 2016).

— (2016) 'What is homelessness?'. Online. http://england.shelter.org.uk/get_advice/ homelessness/homelessness_-_an_introduction/what_is_homelessness (accessed 12 December 2016).

Sparkes, J., and Unwin, J. (2016) 'Foreword'. In Fitzpatrick, S., Pawson, H., Bramley, G., Wilcox, S., and Watts, B. *The Homelessness Monitor: England 2016*. London: Crisis, vi.

Stein, M. (2006) 'Research review: Young people leaving care'. *Child and Family Social Work*, 11 (3): 273–9.

Stone, V., Cotton, D., and Thomas, A. (2000) *Mapping Troubled Lives: Young people not in education, employment or training* (Research Brief 181). Nottingham: DfEE.

Taylor, S.E., Klein, L.C., Lewis, B.P., Gruenewald T.L., Gurung, R.A.R., and Updegraff, J.A. (2000) 'Biobehavioral responses to stress in females: Tend-and-befriend, not fight-or-flight'. *Psychological Review*, 107 (3): 411–29.

Tevendale, H.D., Comulada, W.S. and Lightfoot, M.A. (2011) 'Finding shelter: Two-year housing trajectories among homeless youth'. *Journal of Adolescent Health*, 49 (6): 615–20.

Thomson, P. (2016) 'An ethics of analysis and writing'. Online. https://patthomson. net/2016/12/12/an-ethics-of-analysis-and-writing/ (accessed 14 December 2016).

Tripp, J.H., and Cockett, M. (1998) 'Parents, parenting, and family breakdown'. *Archives of Disease in Childhood*, 78 (2): 104–8.

Turner, R., Irwin, C., and Millstein, S. (1991) 'Family structure, family processes, and experimenting with substances during adolescence'. *Journal of Research on Adolescence*, 1 (1): 93–106.

Umunna, C. (2007) 'In our inner cities, gangs are the new extended families'. *The Guardian*, 9 August. Online. www.theguardian.com/commentisfree/2007/ aug/09/comment.society (accessed 18 May 2015).

United Nations (1948) Universal Declaration of Human Rights. Online. www. ohchr.org/EN/UDHR/Documents/UDHR_Translations/eng.pdf (accessed 19 March 2017).

Van der Ploeg, J.D. (1989) 'Homelessness: A multidimensional problem'. *Children and Youth Services Review*, 11 (1): 45–56.

Walsh, M.E. (1992) 'Moving to Nowhere': Children's stories of homelessness. New York: Auburn House.

Warner, R.L. (2006) 'Being a good parent'. In Gubrium, J.F. and Holstein, J.A. (eds) *Couples, Kids, and Family Life*. New York: Oxford University Press, 65–83.

Watson, J.S. (1999) 'Individual choice and family loyalty: Suzanne Fisher Staples' protagonists come of age'. *ALAN Review*, 27 (1): 25–8. Online. http://scholar. lib.vt.edu/ejournals/ALAN/fall99/watson.html (accessed 4 March 2017).

Watts, B., Johnsen, S., and Sosenko, F. (2015) 'Youth homelessness in the UK: A review for the OVO Foundation'. Institute for Social Policy, Housing, Environment and Real Estate (I-SPHERE), Heriot-Watt University.

Webb, J., Schirato, T. and Danaher, G. (2002) *Understanding Bourdieu*. Crows Nest, NSW: Allen and Unwin.

Wedge, P., and Prosser, H. (1973) *Born to Fail?* London: Arrow Books.

Whalen, A. (2012) 'Developing positive accommodation and support pathways to adulthood: Minimising the risks of youth homelessness and supporting successful transitions for young people'. Online. www.devon.gov.uk/h_ doc12_05_01_13.pdf (accessed 4 March 2017).

Who Cares? Trust (n.d.) 'Leaving care'. Online. www.thewhocarestrust.org.uk/ pages/leaving-care-what-happens-post-16.html (accessed 1 October 2015).

Wilcox, P., Winn, S. and Fyvie-Gauld, M. (2005) '"It was nothing to do with the university, it was just the people": The role of social support in the first-year experience of higher education'. *Studies in Higher Education*, 30 (6): 707–22.

Wiley, A., Rose, A.J., Burger, L.K. and Miller, P.J. (2004) 'Constructing autonomous selves through narrative practices: A comparative study of working-class and middle-class families'. In Shore, C.M. (ed.) *The Many Faces of Childhood: Diversity in development*. Boston: Pearson Education, 99–120.

Wilkinson, R., and Pickett, K. (2010) *The Spirit Level: Why equality is better for everyone*. Rev. ed. London: Penguin Books.

Wilson, W. (2016) 'Applying as homeless from an assured shorthold tenancy' (England) (Briefing Paper 06856). London: House of Commons Library.

Wright, C., and Jagger, G. (1999) 'End of century, end of family? Shifting discourses of family "crisis"'. In Jagger, G., and Wright, C. (eds) *Changing Family Values*. London: Routledge, 17–37.

Wright, C., Standen, P. and Patel, T. (2010) *Black Youth Matters: Transitions from school to success*. London: Routledge.

Index

Index